D1462433

Unions in Postindustrial Society

Unions in Postindustrial Society

John Schmidman

The Pennsylvania State University Press
University Park and London

Library of Congress Cataloging in Publication Data

Schmidman, John.
  Unions in postindustrial society.
  Includes bibliography and index.
  1. Trade-unions—History. 2. Trade-unions—
Service industries workers. I. Title.
HD6476.S33   331.88'09   78-11229
ISBN 0-271-00209-3

Printed in the United States of America

*This book is sincerely dedicated
to Randy Fagin and Steve Rozmus,
who represent our hopes for the future.*

Contents

Preface

The beginnings of this book can be traced back to the early 1970s when I was teaching a course in theories of the labor movement. I was unable to find anything resembling an appropriate text for this course and resorted to preparing a series of readings for my students. During this process I came to the conclusion that a new explanation of trade union structure and function in modern society was called for, but unavailable.

An extensive search of the theoretical works available revealed that they could be divided into two categories: (1) those that emanated during the beginnings of industrialization and corporate development and (2) more recent works seeking to update studies which had become anachronistic or offering new perspectives of their own. Even the latter, however, failed to take into account the dramatic developments in production and the structure of the labor force which took place in the evolution from industrial to postindustrial society.

In this book I have attempted to follow a logical pattern, both chronologically and in terms of issues raised. Chapter 1 deals with the changed environment in which American unions and workers operate—an environment in which the tertiary sector predominates, with every indication of future growth at both an arithmetic and geometric rate. Thus the problem will become even more critical for American workers and their organizations, as well as for the workers and unions of other Western democracies, as they undergo the transformation into postindustrialism. The works of the "early" theorists of the labor movement are discussed in Chapter 2, followed by more recent attempts in Chapter 3. These representative theories are presented without editorial comment, which is presented in the following chapters along with a model of trade unionism in postindustrial society.

The statements made in Chapters 4 through 7 are based on the best data available, over two hundred years of trade union history, the industrial roles of trade unions and collective bargaining, and the works of the theorists already mentioned.

The definitive nature of some of the predictions made, especially in Chapter 4, may bother individuals who, like me, are institutionalists by nature. I too am troubled by the lack of absolute empirical data which would further reinforce these projections. However, the evidence that would satisfy us simply does not exist; the data are not available at this time. Thus, the logical, step-by-step presentation is meant to develop "a," not "the," theory of the labor movement in postindustrial society. The veracity of this model will be tested over the next two decades by myself and others.

Acknowledgments

I am deeply indebted to the Pennsylvania State University for providing me with the sabbatical leave which was necessary for the completion of this manuscript, and to Professor Helmut J. Golatz for his critical role in helping me obtain this leave of absence. Professor Gerald G. Eggert provided invaluable assistance in directing me to appropriate sources dealing with economic history and prevented numerous errors of omission and commission. Mr. Arthur P. Lewandowski of the Office and Professional Employees International Union, AFL-CIO, read an early draft of this manuscript, and his enthusiasm for it came at a time when it was vitally needed. Ms. Mitzi Dailey provided invaluable assitance in assembling the final and earlier versions of this document, and to call her help merely typing would be an injustice. Mr. John M. Pickering, editorial director of The Pennsylvania State University Press, was a constant source of encouragement and provided the type of challenge which every author should be fortunate enough to receive from an editor. Finally, I must mention that during the course of finishing the final version of this manuscript I was fortunate enough to marry Carol Mulhollen Schmidman. Her encouragement at the expense of what marital counselors prescribe as the appropriate beginnings for a happy and successful marriage made the completion of this book both possible and more rewarding than it would have been in her absence.

1

The Postindustrial Era

Organized labor has always had societal power far exceeding its actual numbers and the percentage of the labor force which it has organized. This is the direct result of its economic organization, which has given it a power base from which to exert influence on the economy and on the polity. The need for such a base, arising from the crucial role that economic power has always played in American society, is a lesson that dates back to the early craft unions of the American Federation of Labor.

In fact, the history of organized labor throughout the nineteenth century focuses on two major themes: (1) economic versus political ends and means and (2) the search for an organizational model. Prior to the creation of the AFL and its member unions, organized labor turned toward politics during periods of economic recession and depression. Since the early American unions* were unable to create an organizational model which could survive in both good and bad times, they saw their membership swell during periods of economic prosperity only to be depleted in economic downturns.

The early craft unionists of the AFL looked at history and saw the failure of reform-oriented forms of unionism. Indeed, their immediate predecessor as the major American labor organization—the Knights of Labor—failed because its leaders were unable to translate their ideas for "pie in the sky" into the here-and-now needs of the American worker. They could also consider the experience of the National Labor Union, which had atrophied when it turned political and reformist.

The secret that the AFL unionists discovered was the essentiality of economic power in the functioning of American society. Rather than turn toward politics when the economy took a downturn, they entrenched themselves economically and awaited the next upswing in the economic cycle. Thus they

*The terms union and trade union are used synonymously throughout this book.

avoided internal struggles because of the differing political ideologies of their membership; but more than that, they recognized the primacy of economic power both as a means and as an end.

> Economic betterment—today, tomorrow, in home and shop, was the foundation upon which trade unions have been builded. Economic power is the basis upon which may be developed power in other fields. It is the foundation of organized society. Because I early grasped this fundamental truth, I was never deluded or led astray by rosy theory or fascinating plan that did not square with my fundamental.[1]

The model of trade unionism which was finally able to establish itself firmly in the fiber of American society was based on the craft performed by a certain group of workers. The heterogeneity of the American work force, the broad differences in secular and religious ideologies, and the lack of a class or feudal tradition all contributed to its success; job-related issues provided the glue that held together an otherwise disparate union movement.

The leaders of the early AFL craft unions based their economic power on the control of the supply of skilled labor. Since the apprenticeship program required by the skilled trades meant that these artisans could not easily be replaced, a power base was thus created which no politician, no legislature, and no court could erode. While the leaders of these unions expressed sympathy for unskilled and semiskilled labor, they felt that such workers were incapable of establishing permanent organizations because they were so easily replaced.

The member unions of the American Federation of Labor received a boost in their bargaining efforts during World War I. Organized labor's cooperation was essential if the domestic war effort was to proceed unimpeded, and collective bargaining flourished. With the end of hostilities, however, employers took the offensive and began an attack on both trade unions and collective bargaining. The principle of organizing according to craft or skill proved unable to organize mass-production industries. The combination of these two factors with the issuance of injunctions by federal courts in cases arising out of labor disputes caused organized labor to decline in membership from about three million to slightly less than two million members during the 1920s.

The Capitalistic/Industrial Era

The late 1800s and early 1900s saw the triumph of what Mathew Josephson has called the "robber barons," as the captains of industry took over from the captains of finance in controlling the economy. This period also saw the increasing dominance of the machine as the major means of production.

> Among the basic industries iron and steel were essentially machine produced. Bridgebuilding, shipbuilding, the manufacture of iron pipe and steel wire had become mechanized. Lathes, planes, drilling machines, grinding machines, trip hammers, and hydro-electric presses had taken over the foundries. Copper refining and the production of virgin aluminum, lead, zinc, silver, and cement had become largely machine produced.[2]

Throughout this transitional decade in the development of American industry, enterprises grew rapidly in size and scale as the technology of production improved. The triumph of the factory system coincided with the triumph of capitalism, for, just as the industrial society depends on energy, there is a corresponding reliance on the capitalistic system as the method of distributing and investing the fruits of industrial production.

The key characteristic of the labor force in capitalistic/industrial society is the large numbers and percentage of workers employed in manufacturing as opposed to agricultural and/or extraction-type occupations. At the height of the industrial era, about two-thirds of the American labor force consisted of employees in some type of manufacturing industry.

Meanwhile, the application of industrial techniques enabled a smaller percentage of the total labor force to produce a larger absolute number of agricultural products. With farming becoming a big business, individuals left the land and migrated to urban areas where manufacturing was booming. During the 1920s, when rural depression was coupled with relative industrial prosperity, the trend toward urbanization became pronounced. The migration into the cities and into the factories resulted in the blending of a conservative rural viewpoint with the outlook of the urbanized immigrant workers and the attitude of various ethnic and racial groups.

The business enterprise was fast becoming the focal institution in American society. It was also autonomous, having "its own law and rationale in its function."[3] The rapid growth and concentration of American business and industry was, in fact, the major feature of the 1920s;[4] in this respect the decade prior to the Great Depression can be compared to the years just before and after the turn of the century.

The term "people's capitalism" became a much-used phrase, reflecting the theory that the ordinary citizen could share the fruits of the capitalistic system through stock ownership.[5] It was during this period that the divorce between ownership and the control of American industry began. "Because ownership was widely diffused, the managers became a self-perpetuating group that was more or less free to shape the corporation's future so long as the managers were not guilty of any unseemly conduct that might arouse stockholder ire."[6] At the same time, management was "becoming both professional and scientific."[7]

There was another side to this panacea of people's capitalism: the alarming concentration of corporate power, documented in the hearings of the Temporary National Economic Committee. While the number of individual stockholders did increase dramatically, it is important to remember that the great majority of stock was concentrated in fewer and fewer hands.[8] In the late 1920s, "1 per cent of the investors received about 70 per cent of the dividends."[9]

Postcapitalism and Industrial Unionism

With the advent of the Great Depression of 1929 and the start of President Franklin D. Roosevelt's New Deal, the capitalistic system which had existed in the United States underwent a drastic alteration. The most novel aspect of the New Deal was the new involvement of the federal government in the attempt to deal with the country's severe economic problems. While previously the role of the federal government in the economy had been mostly regulatory (and even then only to a modest extent), President Roosevelt believed that the government should play an active, affirmative part in fighting the ravages of the depression and redistributing wealth and income. "In other words, economic planning was to replace the philosophy of laissez faire,"[10] which had proved itself inadequate.

> It is not surprising that peacetime economic planning became popular, for conditions in the United States presented a sorry and perplexing picture. Thousands of persons were going hungry while farmers were plagued by huge surpluses of grain and meat. Actually, people were starving amidst abundance. There were millions of unemployed workers, billions of idle capital, and great quanti-

ties of raw materials; yet these factors of production were not being used to supply the needs of the people. America had the resources to provide an abundant life for all and seemed only to lack an intelligent plan of action.[11]

There was no single New Deal philosophy; rather, the program stemmed from many individuals representing many different philosophies. Most of the pieces of legislation which served as the New Deal's experiments to achieve economic recovery were designed to benefit the population generally. Among these can be included the National Industrial Recovery Act, the Social Security Act, the Emergency Banking Act, and the Fair Labor Standards Act. Others sought to benefit a specific geographical section of the country or a particular sector of the population. These included the Tennessee Valley Authority, the Civilian Conservation Corps, and the Agricultural Adjustment Act. With the exception of Section 7(a) of the National Industrial Recovery Act, the only piece of New Deal legislation which sought to advance the interests of organized labor was the National Labor Relations (Wagner) Act of 1935. The Wagner Act protected workers in their right to join and form unions, imposed upon employers a duty to bargain with the chosen representative of their employees, and set up the machinery (the National Labor Relations Board) to administer the act.

Meanwhile, a split was taking place within the ranks of organized labor between the advocates of industrial versus craft unionism. Within the AFL, the Committee for Industrial Organization (CIO) was formed, advocating one large union for each mass-production industry. In 1935, a break occurred, and the Committee for Industrial Organization became a separate labor federation—the Congress of Industrial Organizations.

The two groups differed strikingly in their attitudes toward government. The anachronistic ideology of the AFL was a hangover from the days of capitalism. Its leaders preferred to make gains through collective bargaining rather than through governmental action or intervention, fearing that what one government gave another government could take away. Also, they were anxious lest workers begin to look toward government for benefits rather than looking toward their trade unions.

From the start, the unions making up the CIO did not suffer from the same fear of government intervention as did their AFL counterparts. They were to benefit greatly from the rulings of the National Labor Relations Board during this post-capitalistic but industrial era, especially as regards the board's determinations of the units appropriate for bargaining. (A bargaining unit is any group of employees with a mutuality of interest in wages, hours, and other terms and conditions of employment.)

When Edwin S. Smith and William M. Leiserson formed a two-member majority on the NLRB, they reasoned that, since it was the policy of the federal government to foster trade unionism and collective bargaining, in a *ceteris paribus* situation regarding the appropriateness of a proposed bargaining unit, they would make that decision according to what would most greatly enhance the bargaining power of labor. In applying this measure, they felt that the unit which gave the workers the greatest bargaining power vis-à-vis management was a wall-to-wall or industrial unit. Thus the NLRB ruled as appropriate those units in which the mutuality of interest between the employees was the fact that they worked for the same employer, and ruled out units in which the mutuality or commonality of interest was a skill or type of job. In opting for industrial units, the board gave a boost to the organizing efforts of the CIO unions.[12] Faced with this situation, the AFL affiliates emulated their counterparts in the CIO and organized industrially. This was done in two ways: (1) their already existing affiliates organized industrially and (2) the federation chartered new industrial unions of their own to rival the unions of the CIO.

All these activities occurred in an era which can be described as both postcapitalistic and industrial; for while the role of government in the economy had changed, the primacy of industrial production continued, and a majority of the labor force was still employed in industry. The carry-over of industrial organization from this era which began to see its demise with the close of World War II still haunts the trade union movement today. It is one of the major difficulties which organized labor must face if it is not to see its power diminished in postindustrial society.

The Beginnings of the Postindustrial Era

The postindustrial era in the United States began at the end of World War II, and centers around the functioning of an economy which is more service oriented than goods oriented.

It is possible to discern at this stage a transition to an economy in which the majority of the labor force is employed in nonmanufacturing positions, the so-called tertiary sector of the economy.

The proportion of the labor force employed in the agricultural sector of the economy shrinks to a small percentage of the total work force. In fact, some would claim that the major shift in the employment of the labor force is not from manufacturing to service employment but rather from agriculture to service employment;[13] however, the move away from agricultural employment began in the industrial era and is further accentuated in the postindustrial era. This shift creates a market for goods and services connected with agriculture, thus adding to both the industrial and service portions of the economy.

To explain the dramatic nature of the changes in the composition of the labor force, it is necessary to take into account the rapid increase in the demand for services. This occurs because there is a direct relationship between the rise in real income and the demand for services; that is, the consumer demand for services rises faster than the demand for goods.[14] But employment in the service sector is labor intensive, not capital intensive. This accounts for the rise in the real numbers of tertiary employees.

At the start of the postindustrial era, industrial conflict has become institutionalized, for every act of organization is also an act of institutionalization. Rather than assuming destructive forms, industrial conflict has assumed constructive forms through collective bargaining. The nature of collective bargaining causes conflict between employer and employee/ employee representative to become centered or isolated around job-related issues. Industrial conflict and its resolution have become separated from political conflict; for instead of seeking the transformation of the entire society in which they exist, trade unions have developed narrower goals which can be accomplished through the mechanisms of collective bargaining.[15] Thus the working class obtains a stake in the *status quo*.

The shift in the structure of employment creates certain problems for organized labor. Especially since the advent of industrial organization, the major source of labor's strength has been the unions in the large, mass-production industries along with unions of goods-producing workers in general. Unions have not met with the same degree of success in organizing service or white-collar employees. While organized labor has grown in absolute numbers, it has not increased dramatically as a percentage of the labor force since the end of World War II. Some individuals would have us believe that unions have reached a "plateau" or extent of organization and thus the boundary of their societal strength.[16] This "plateau" argument was made, however, before the great upsurge in union organization among public employees at all levels, federal, state, and local. While the claim has been made that public-employee unions are "built on a base of sand," they have in fact provided a new source of vitality within the American trade union movement.

It is not inconceivable that the same surge of organization which one finds among unions of public employees will occur in the tertiary sector. The key to this possibility of organization is the structure of an employment relationship; for this, like economic disaster,* is one of the stimuli to which American workers have reacted in organizing for the purpose of collective bargaining. The different roles of order givers and order takers in the relatively affluent service sector will likely cause the informal conflict inherent in all employment situations to take a formalized, that is unionized, form. The rising concern of organized labor with this situation further increases the likelihood that the message of the benefits of collective bargaining will reach these employees who were previously considered impossible or difficult to organize.

Trade Union Autonomy and Economic Planning

While it can be said that the United States is the only postindustrial nation in the world, it must be added that the economies of other countries are headed in the same direction (though their evolution into postindustrial societies is several years off). All these nations are economic and political democracies, and all have autonomous trade union movements, for it is only in democratic economies that one finds trade union autonomy, rather than unions acting as the official wing of the ruling party or government.

This autonomy breeds a contempt for monoliths, and the pluralism present in such countries lends itself to a situation in

---

*This would include phenomena such as the Great Depression and World Wars I and II. See Bernstein, "The Growth of American Unions."

which parochial interest groups are able to seek their own self-serving interests. Such economic pluralism is a necessary correlate of postindustrialism. A postcapitalistic/postindustrial society is a planned society. This economic planning is of the indicative rather than the imperative type, involving the government and the vested interest groups, namely labor and management. No one party, not even the government, has the final or determining say in the structure or operation of the planning process (in contrast to the imperative planning found in Marxist countries, where the government plays the major or only decision-making role).[17]

A formalized planning apparatus of the type indicated does not currently exist in the United States, but this does not negate its inevitability in the future. What will likely occur in this country is the slow development of a sanctioned planning structure. This may take the form of "pluralistic industrialism" in which the state does not "wither away"[18] but assumes the role of mediating the conflict between the managers and the managed, setting rights and responsibilities.

It is perhaps ironic that indicative economic planning occurs in the industrial societies of Western Europe rather than in the postindustrial United States. It must be remembered, however, that the necessity for some form of economic planning in Western Europe dates back to the termination of World War II, when it was more a matter of economic necessity than a stage of postindustrial development. In the United States, the role of public versus private planning has always been more uncertain than it has in Western Europe. Historically, we have had more government by bargaining than government by planning, and this custom has carried over in spite of the changes and experiments dating back to the New Deal. Public authority has remained fragmented, and individual "interest groups and other organized bodies inside and outside government tend instinctively to separate themselves off from the rest and to function as autonomous entities."[19] This experience in the United States strengthens the argument that only autonomous trade union movements are able to exert pressure on the economy, the polity, and the society in general. At any rate, when economic planning in the postindustrial United States does take place, it will assume a form which differs from that in Western Europe as the result of historical traditions and the imperatives of postindustrialism.

Certainly another reason for the existence of planning in Western Europe is the political traditions of the trade unions in these nations. The labor movements in these countries started out as three-pronged affairs, consisting of a trade union movement, a cooperative movement, and a labor, socialist or social democratic party. Reformistic goals such as universal male suffrage and free public education were won by around 1840 in the United States but were not achieved until somewhere around the turn of the century in Western Europe. When these reforms were won, they came about through a collective political effort. The interrelationship of economics and politics in Western European trade union movements, along with their commitment to the complete transformation of capitalistic society, made their endorsement of and participation in forms of national economic planning a more natural occurrence.[20]

In contrast, trade unions in the postindustrial United States are likely to endorse and take part in national economic planning as a defensive reaction rather than because of any commitment to a "transformed" or "utopian" society. The imperatives of such an economic system will create the necessity for a rational planning process in which organized labor will have a vested interest. The unions will be able to make their presence felt because of the base of economic power which has been created through collective bargaining. This very success of collective bargaining has made workers operating through their unions part of the vested interests in American society, and contractual gains have coincided with legislative gains. The transformation to postindustrialism will threaten this vested interest in much the same way that the gains which unions have made for their membership have been threatened in the past.

Since the initial triumphs of the early AFL affiliates, organized labor has been faced with both economic and political challenges to the gains which it has made through collective bargaining. The reaction of the craft unions was to shun politics and concentrate on economic actions. The reaction of the CIO affiliates was to become involved in the political process, and this example was quickly emulated by their AFL counterparts. Today the AFL-CIO has an active legislative program to protect the gains that have already been won from erosion by the legislatures and the courts. The relationship between this legislative program of an autonomous trade union movement and the existence of a more active form of economic planning will result in both a different type of political involvement and a new relationship between organized labor and the government.

Labor will increasingly become involved in policy-making decisions. The centralized structure of some unions easily lends itself to this process; for others, participation will call for extreme structural changes. Internal political power tends to reside at the level in a union at which collective bargaining takes place. In large industrial unions where the national executive engages in bargaining with large corporations, power within the union tends to be disproportionately found at the national level. In unions containing a large percentage, or majority, of skilled workers, power tends to reside at the regional or local level, because bargaining occurs at these lower levels of the union hierarchy. It is in this latter case that the transition to economic planning will be the most difficult, since decentralized bargaining does not lend itself to national economic planning or the development of an incomes policy. While the National Joint Board for settling jurisdictional disputes nationally and locally in the construction industry has operated successfully for several years, disparity in negotiated agreements does exist according to geographical location.

This restructuralization will be forced upon unions if they are to participate in economic planning in the postindustrial era. As is shown by the efforts at coordinated bargaining on the part of unions working through the Industrial Union Department of the AFL-CIO, these organizations already relinquish some of their autonomy to effectively face the conglomerate or multiindustry employer. A comparable and even more extensive effect on trade union autonomy will result from economic planning. The difficulty for unions will be in discovering a balance between this participation and their primary task of representing the job-related interests of their membership. Unions serve a restricted clientele, and are not meant to contribute directly to the betterment of society. Union officials are elected to service the members who elect them, and "unions exist to serve their own interests, not someone else's."[21]

This dilemma between trade union autonomy and national economic planning in postindustrial society will find its resolution in the development of a two-tiered union structure. First, unions must continue to perform the vital function of institutionalizing or channelling conflict inherent in any employment situation at the local or work-site level. This conflict will not disappear; it will be dealt with gradually and flexibly. In spite of the cooperation which exists between management and labor at this level, the very nature of the authority relationship means that this function of trade unionism is essential to all its other activities. This institutionalization of conflict serves to stabilize one aspect of the employing enterprise; it is self-defeating for a union to end an employment relationship by forcing an employer out of existence. "It is of benefit to nobody to perform a hysterectomy on the goose that lays the golden eggs."[22]

On the other hand, trade unions will find themselves serving on major decision-making entities which will call for increased responsibility on their part. They will be asked to perform functions that have not existed in the past. The result may be the development of a gap between these two levels of unionism and the union officials who function at these seemingly contradictory levels. The primary function of unions makes participation at this national policy-making level all the more difficult, but this does not mean that these attempts will fail. What it does mean is that trade unions will be increasingly integrated into the functioning of postindustrial society, and that they will play an even more vital role in the future governing of society.[23]

Political Democracy

The success which pluralistic political democracy has achieved in the United States will assist in blunting some of the negative political aspects of the concentration of power which accompanies evolution into postindustrial society. The history of the relationship between organized labor and the polity lends credence to this optimism. Incidents of political conflict or crisis have brought labor into the political arena; but once these political crises have been resolved, organized labor has not disappeared from the scene. Such victories have seldom been complete. There have always been new adversaries to contend with and new battles to be fought. This is the essence of pluralistic democracy.

Political conflict which is external to the organization has traditionally produced trade union cohesion. The threat need not even actually exist; it needs only to be perceived to produce this result. The same is true of nonlabor groups operating in a democracy. Single-issue interest groups disappear once that issue is obtained, but political pressure groups which are able to define their goals and aspirations broadly and flexibly find themselves able to transcend the built-in self-destruct mechanisms of ephemeral organizations. This ability to struggle against new antagonists in the political arena is essential if an interest group is to maintain its societal strength.

Conflict in the political arena tends to serve as a unifier for the organizations taking part in the pressure group process. If a postindustrial society allows this conflict to exist in an unstructured fashion, it runs the risk of allowing these tensions to tear apart the very fiber of organized society. Government must play the role of referee between political antagonists, in much the same way as it mediates between labor and management. Failure to do so will produce chaos and anarchy, which will neutralize the multiple and tangible benefits to be gained from postindustrialism. The function of government is to establish rules and regulations to administer this new form of political conflict.[24]

> Conflicts may be said to be "productive" in two related ways: (1) they lead to the modification and the creation of law; (2) the application of new rules leads to the growth of new institutional structures centering on the enforcement of these new rules and laws.[25]

Postindustrial society will result in a proliferation of parochial interest groups, each seeking its own interests. This is not inconsistent with the concentration of economic power which takes place in the industrial sector; but unlike this industrial concentration, which leads to political concentration, a service-oriented economy allows individuals and groups on the fringe of organized political power to make their existence felt in the political arena. A service-oriented economy offers and creates the need for collective bargaining among the formerly economically disenfranchised. It creates a new generation of employees who have not previously thought of bargaining as a means of improving their on-the-job and hence their off-the-job status. The politically alienated Americans who have played the role of the disillusioned of industrial society[26] will find their political power increasing because of the use of these basic economic methods to improve their status in society.

This tendency is further augmented by the expansion of government as employer. Employment in government, especially at the state and local levels, has grown more rapidly than in any other sector of the American economy. In the decade of the 1960s, governmental employment increased at nearly two and one-half times the growth rate for total employment elsewhere in the economy. By 1980, it is predicted that 16.8 million Americans will be government employees, "up from 11.8 million in 1968."[27] In spite of the fact that government has always thought of itself as a model employer, collective bargaining is expanding at a phenomenal rate in the public sector. The result will be a new trade union movement resembling the new labor force. Collective bargaining will replace anachronistic civil service systems, and the bilateral determination of wages, salaries, hours, and conditions of employment will replace the former unilateralism. This will also result in a new and potent political force being added to the ranks of organized labor. The expansion of collective bargaining in both the private and public sectors of the service economy creates the potential for a revitalized economic power base serving as the cornerstone of a politically renovated trade union movement.

The outsiders will become insiders. Recognizing the essentiality of the possession of an economic power base as the key for broader political and societal change, the challengers will find that the "rules of pluralistic politics" are not self-defeating once they define their goals more narrowly so as to make them achievable. In spite of the argument that pluralistic theory cannot be applied to members and nonmembers of the polity,[28] postindustrialism will allow contestants to exercise the influence they seek if they have the will and boldness to do so.

2

The Industrial Theorists

In order to understand the functioning and role of trade unions in postindustrial society, it is first necessary to know the goals which labor pursued in industrial society and the means they used to achieve these ends. In this chapter we examine some of the first theories describing or prescribing the evolution, functions, and operation of trade unions. It should be noted that all of them arose during the era of *laissez-faire* capitalism, and all are profoundly influenced by the repercussions of the industrial revolution. In other words, as is true of all total or partial theories, they are the products of their environment.

An attempt has been made to present the broadest possible spectrum of theorists of the labor movement in industrial society. The opposing explanations of Norman J. Ware and Selig Perlman are followed by a summary of Richard T. Ely's Christian socialism. John R. Commons's expansion-of-markets theory is evolutionary in perspective, and Frank Tannenbaum's two major works on the subject, while they differ in their treatment of the revolutionary nature of trade unionism, also offer a historical perspective.

Robert F. Hoxie offers a view of trade union structure and a somewhat psychological treatment of trade union functional types. Sidney and Beatrice Webb focus on the origins of trade unionism and expand their perspective to include the different methods which unions used to achieve their ends. Although they referred specifically to British society, their works can be and have been applied to the American situation. The chapter closes with an account of Karl Marx's writings on the unfolding of the capitalist system of production and capitalist society in general. In Marx's dialectic model, unions can do very little to alter the inevitable. Lenin updated Marx, however, developing a context within which unions could play a strategic role in the class struggle.

Norman J. Ware[1]

Norman J. Ware's basic premise was that prior to the depression of 1837–1840 workers maintained a degree of independence from the job market, and consequently had some voice in community affairs. This situation was drastically altered in the 1840s, however, by the development of the factory system. "The problem of primary importance for the industrial worker of the forties and fifties is to be found in the changes in his status and standards of living" (*IW*, p. 26).

Before the 1840s, according to Ware, the worker's income was based on "price," the remuneration he received for the sale of the end product of his labor. The payment of wages came about through the introduction of machinery into a factory, with accompanying job specialization. As previously existing skills were broken down, the competition for these factory jobs increased. The specter of unemployment began to haunt the American worker.

> The change of status involved in the transfer to the factory system is best seen in the character of unemployment. In domestic production, unemployment meant leisure and a change of work—a change that was often pleasant and sometimes profitable. But as trade specialization and urban conditions developed, unemployment spelled increasingly want and discontent. (*IW*, p. 39)

The industrial worker was degraded by the industrial revolution. With the accumulation of capital, the factory workers lost their independence and with it their dignity. Thus the controversy over employment conditions in the factories themselves missed the crux of the matter. The dehumanization to which the factory worker objected lay in the system itself.

Ware saw two main characteristics of the industrial revolution in the United States: (1) the application of machinery to production via the factory system and (2) transfer of sovereignty in economic affairs from the community as a whole to a special class. The protests of the industrial workers were centered around the second phenomenon and, during the 1840s, took a defensive form as the workers sought to cling to the traditions and methods of the past. In this protest they were joined by the social reformers of the era; the two groups "came together as one" (*IW*, p. 199) to cry out against the same phenomenon. Both workers and reformers, however, failed to recognize the inevitability of the industrial revolution and its ramifications.

By 1850, the reaction of workers to industrialization had changed. The labor movement of the previous decade had "represented the worker as a citizen of a community rather than a member of a craft" (*IW*, p. 227). The emerging labor movement, however, recognized employers and employed as groups with different interests and determined to strive for their own benefit within the work situation. Accepting the loss of status resulting from the industrial revolution, the workers in the fifties sought to organize around their crafts for the purpose of bargaining collectively with their employers. (Some did experiment with the ideas of producers' cooperatives and political action; but these were exclusive organizations concerned with the condition of their own members and crafts, not with the labor movement as a whole.) The unions were largely unsuccessful in their efforts, and the labor movement wound up the decade of the 1860s as impotent as it had been at the start of the industrial revolution in the United States in 1840 (*IW*, pp. 227–40).

In his study of early unionism Ware was particularly interested in the Knights of Labor. He felt that the Knights appreciated the lesson taught the labor movement by the industrial revolution—that technology had wiped out job distinctions based on craft, and that worker solidarity, not craft particularism, offered the only hope for workers in combating the large industrial corporation. The problem which the organization faced early in its existence was how to translate the ideal of solidarity into tangible forms (*LM*, p. 156).

The Knights were, in fact, constantly torn between the notions of labor solidarity and craft organization. Even though they realized the effectiveness of class solidarity as the inevitable response to the changes in the methods of production which American industry had undergone, they were unable to develop this unity because of their inept leadership. The *coup de grace* in this respect occurred when the leaders failed to call a retreat in order to regroup after the failure of the eight-hour movement in 1888 (*LM*, pp. 299–319).

Ware discerned four main streams in the evolution of the American labor movement: (1) fraternalism, (2) collective bargaining, (3) cooperation, and (4) politics (*LM*, p. 320). The triumph of collective bargaining as a means to labor's ends was due to the early leadership of the American Federation of Labor and its member unions, and particularly to the activities of Samuel Gompers, the first president of the AFL.

Gompers was aware of labor's tenuous situation in 1888 and withdrew into the safety of craft exclusiveness. In so doing, Ware believed, Gompers betrayed the ideal of labor leadership by teaching that a worker's primary identity is that of a wage earner. However, Ware did not feel that class consciousness was disappearing. He assumed that the end of the free land of the frontier and the ascendancy of "large-scale production" would freeze the American worker into a wage-earning class from which there could be no escape, and that this fixed status would increase both class consciousness and the solidarity of labor.

In *Labor in Modern Industrial Society,* Ware distinguishes between two basic types of philosophies of labor which transcend what he views as apparent, but not real, differences. Philosophies of the first category repudiate the wage-profit system; those of the second category accept such a system as a fact of life within which workers must operate if they are to promote their own interests (*LMIS,* p. 378).

The same work contains an analysis of the working class and its leaders. Ware holds that the workers' degree of class consciousness is influenced by several factors, the most important being their leadership. Three basic types of labor leader are described: (1) the intellectual, (2) the executive, and (3) the agitator (*LMIS,* p. 34).

Ware identifies intellectuals as labor leaders who come from outside the working class. This type of leader is seen as having far less influence in the United States than in Europe, due in part to the pragmatic attitude of the American people. The ineptitude of the American intellectual is demonstrated by the lack of flexibility in his doctrinaire approach, his grandiose schemes, and his contempt for the "here-and-now" aspirations of the American worker.

The intellectual is also impeded in his programmatic approach by the more acceptable pragmatism of the executive type of labor leader, a type Ware described with Samuel Gompers specifically in mind.

According to Ware, leaders of the executive type were often criticized for four basic "sins": they were exclusively concerned with the interests of the members of their craft unions; they were overly concerned with maintaining their positions and with receiving large salaries; they exhibited class collaboration in their dealings with employers; and they were guilty of racketeering.

In reply to the first charge, Ware notes that concern with the interests of a particular craft is shared by the membership of a craft union, and that this self-concern is a natural expression of all human institutions. As regards the second charge, Ware admits that trade unions are essentially political organizations in spite of their external economic orientation, and governing these organizations comprises a large part of the job of a union leader. However, he distinguishes between obtaining such a position and maintaining it. A union leader must have a "machine" to remain in office, and especially to be reelected. The natural tendency for this type of leader to try to hold on to his privileged position must often run counter to the best interests of the membership and the organization.

As for "class collaboration," the term is actually not appropriate to most union activities in the United States, because it implies a labor movement whose members display class consciousness. Ware thus offered the term "union-management cooperation" as a more appropriate title for this third, and most serious, allegation. He admits that union leaders have to deal with management as part of their essential function, and the charge of cooperation bears credence when such activity is undertaken in behalf of the union leaders and not the union's membership.

Ware distinguishes three phases of the relationship between union and management. The first of these is antagonism, in which either side refuses to deal with the other. Cooperation is the second stage, in which both labor and management act according to their own best interests and their mutual interest. The third phase, conspiracy, is a form of racketeering in which both union and management act to secure their own private gain at the expense of both the individual workers and the firm or industry. This latter situation occurs when employers are in dire financial straits or are unable to afford a work stoppage.

The agitator, Ware's third category of union leader, typically enters strikes once they have already begun. Such a leader appeals chiefly to "alien" workers who are oppressed and looking for an "ism" to alleviate their pitiful situation. While the agitator is able to organize strikes, he is not capable of building lasting labor organizations.

Ware concluded that three variables—economic, ideological, and personal—were responsible for organized labor's course of development. Personal leadership, in particular, had a perva-

sive effect on American labor unions. Of paramount importance was the influence of Samuel Gompers, whose authority
over the labor movement was based both on his personality and
on the machine which he had developed. While Gompers was
recognized as the spokesman for organized labor, he did not
speak for "the mass of American wage-earners" but for trade
union officialdom. Unions were in desperate need of a change
in leadership coming from the rank and file, but this possibility
was not a strong one (*LMIS*, pp. 494–98).

Ware further lamented the possibility of the American labor
movement's ever taking on a socialist bent. To permit this, an
entente would have to be reached between the socialist intellectual and the American worker, and the leadership of organized labor made such an agreement a near impossibility.
Without the support of the mass of workers, the intellectual
and his philosophy are without strength; but at the same
time, "a trade union movement without something larger
than a wages philosophy tends to become sterile" (*LMIS*, p.
379). By overshadowing economic and ideological considera-
tions, the human factor, leadership, had caused this sterility
in the American trade union movement.

Selig Perlman[2]

Following John R. Commons at the University of Wisconsin,
Selig Perlman dealt with both the social history of the trade
union movement and the development of a theory explaining
its evolution and functions. Such a theory, he asserted, had to
include a discussion of the psychology of the worker (pp. 4–5,
237).

Perlman felt that the workers' flirtations with the various
reform movements of the 1800s delayed the development of a
true trade union mentality and philosophy. What was lacking
in the labor movement was a structure and program which
could survive the uncertainties of the business cycle, and this
necessitated an avoidance of middle-class panaceas.[3]

In his development of a theory of trade unionism, Perlman
saw three major historical factors which dominated union development: (1) the resistance power of capitalism, (2) the role
of the intellectual, and (3) the trade union movement itself.

Capitalism is a "social organization with an effective will to
power" Its strength depends on the experience, maturity, and
aggressiveness of the business community. The resistance

power of capitalism is the capability, or incapability, of the capitalists to survive as the ruling faction in a society—their ability to survive the challenge of revolution even without government support.

Anticapitalist sentiments and movements emerge from the intelligentsia. This group envisions labor as an abstract and massive force to be used as a vehicle in their schemes to drastically alter society.

The character and function of the trade union movement is the third factor determining the course of labor history. A mature union movement which follows its own philosophy and engages in a constant fight with employers for "income, security, and liberty" at the job site will be able to resist the programmatic intellectuals who would have labor subservient to their revolutionary goals.

Perlman distinguishes between three types of economic philosophies: those of the manual worker, the businessman, and the intellectual. The businessman is optimistic, has a consciousness of abundance, and is by nature an economic individualist. The worker, on the other hand, has developed a "manualist psychology." He sees himself as existing in a world of limited economic opportunity in which he cannot afford to take risks. The result is pessimism and fear of uncertainty. This manualist psychology permeates all trade union activities: Through their organizations, workers try to make a living in a world in which there are fewer jobs than job seekers and free competition is self-destructive.

> The group then asserts its collective ownership over the whole amount of opportunity, and, having determined who are entitled to claim a share in that opportunity, undertakes to parcel it out fairly, directly or indirectly, among its recognized members, permitting them to avail themselves of such opportunities, job or market, only on the basis of a "common rule." (p. 242)

The mentality of the manual worker leads him to act through his organization to establish a series of working rules which deal with job control and assume an overwhelming importance. The type of union which develops a complete "law of the job" is both stable and mature because its leaders have risen from the ranks of the union's membership. Such a union is capable of serving both the collective will and the individual member because it has developed a "home-grown" philosophy. While it attempts to satisfy the needs of its individual members, it also develops in the member a willingness to subordinate his own interests to those of the group. It creates a type of liberty on the job which is readily visible to the member (pp. 254–79).

What differentiates the trade unionist from the intellectual is the worker's psychological makeup and his view of economic opportunity. Labor's philosophy is organic, basing liberty on job control through a series of rules; Perlman contrasts this with the abstract and remote concept of freedom advocated by socialists of various ilks who wish to impose their ideology on labor. Thus the socialist intellectual advocates workers' control of employment situations. The worker, however, feels incapable of taking upon himself the risks of management and will support only the collective ownership of opportunity (pp. 6–7, 237–47). Perlman dismisses the tendency of the intellectual to turn labor from "prosaic matters" as "social mysticism" (pp. 280–303).

In dealing with the three factors which dominate the development of trade unionism, Perlman explains why job-conscious unionism, rather than the class-conscious unionism of other nations, developed in the United States. The first reason is that the resistance power of capitalism is extremely strong and deeply rooted in American society, and the institution of private property is also deeply entrenched. The conservatism of American society has been tested by several reform and radical labor organizations in this country's history. One hundred years of experience has clearly demonstrated "that under no circumstances can labor afford to arouse the fears of the great middle class for the safety of private property as a basic institution" (p. 160). The result of such action will result in the strongly entrenched middle class allying itself with antiunion employers to restrain or crush the labor movement in any way possible.

Added to this is the absence of a class-conscious labor movement in America, as a result of the availability of free land in the West, individual mobility, the early winning of universal male suffrage, and the heterogeneity of the American population. The consequence is a consciousness which is more limited in scope than that based on class. Job consciousness fills this void. With its rather limited objective of "wage and job control," it has transcended the divisive nature of its environment and has made American unionism the most effective in the world.

The economic nature of the American trade union movement and the "inadequacy" of political action as a means to achieve labor's goals can be traced directly to the pluralism of the American political system. Given the lack of class cohesiveness, which makes a labor party an impossibility, organized labor has used its economic power as a base to protect itself through nonpartisan political activities (pp. 154–76).

Because of this country's special conditions, a new species of labor movement developed in America, largely as the brainchild of three men: Samuel Gompers and Adolph Strasser of the Cigarmakers and Peter J. McGuire of the Carpenters. Prior to the program of the American Federation of Labor, trade union philosophy was largely centered around the cause of antimonopoly struggles, greenbackism, and the single-tax proposals of Henry George. Labor allied itself with other segments of the "producing classes" in the struggle to win power comparable to that of the monopolist. Gompers and Strasser, however, felt that this principle was insufficient to unite the various factions in the trade union movement.

Gompers and his associates came to believe that the only certain method of preventing the disintegration of a trade union was to build it around a job. They "grasped the idea, supremely correct for American conditions, that the economic front was the only front on which the labor army could stay united" (p. 197). In times of economic recession or depression, they would not turn toward politics as their predecessor unionists had done, but would rather entrench themselves economically and await the next opportunity to press forward once again; meanwhile, union benefit programs would keep their members from dropping out. This course of action is comparable to the one which the Webbs envisioned under the method of mutual benefit.

This model of job-conscious unionism assumed limited employment opportunities, and thus sought to establish a degree of ownership over the job and the establishment of a common rule. Where outright ownership was impossible, these unionists sought to control the labor supply by establishing rights in the jobs through collective bargaining. The resulting concept of industrial democracy envisioned a series of rules, established jointly by employers and unions, which applied to all workers. This model of unionism fit both the external environment in which these organizations existed and the scarcity consciousness of the workers. Recognizing the conservative nature of American society, job-conscious unionism acknowledged the limited effectiveness of political action, and the result was the first stable form of American trade unionism.

This development accounts for the absence of a labor party in the United States. Perlman states a further reason: that social-welfare legislation had been passed because it was successfully demonstrated that the protection of the lower echelons of the social and economic strata is within the meaning of the policing power of the state as defined by the Constitution. This fact reduces the motivation to form a labor party; and if one were to be created the federal structure of the American political system would necessitate a multiplicity of political activity at both the national and state levels. This makes the attainment of political power "beset with difficulties."

The differences among American political parties are not based on class distinctions; furthermore, the party system predates the division of labor and capital. Many of the proposals adopted by "class" parties have been coopted as part of the program of existing political parties. Additionally, the American worker has felt a deep attachment toward the existing political parties which would be difficult to overcome. Unlike the intellectual, the trade union leader does not feel at home in political activities. His arena of struggle is on the economic front.[4]

Perlman also applied what he termed the three dominant factors which emerge from labor history to the labor movements of three countries in addition to the United States: Russia, Germany, and England. The variations in the power of these three variables were used to explain the differing development of trade unions in these countries, especially in contrast to the American experience.

Although Perlman devised a scheme of trade unionism to fit his own times, his theory is noteworthy for its longevity. It attracted praise, attack, and criticism for many years after its conception, and it still does so today.

Richard T. Ely[5]

The years 1880 to 1900 saw the development of Christian socialism in the United States. Unlike comparable movements in Europe American Christian socialism did not prescribe affiliation with any specific church. Starting from the concept of ethical and moral improvement as essential for eventual salvation, the movement in the United States moved quickly toward an emphasis on such uplift as essential for the greatest possible individual satisfaction during one's physical life. Foremost among the Christian socialists in the United States was Richard T. Ely.

Ely envisioned the labor movement as the systematic struggle of the great mass of workers to obtain their primary goals of increased leisure and economic enhancement. But this was only part of the struggle for "a richer existence . . . with respect to mind, soul, and body" (p. 3). The labor movement was the major force fighting for the attainment of the capacity for good in mankind. It pressed not merely for self-improvement, but for the betterment of others as well. Directed against oppression, it sought the peaceful development of a society in which all individuals could find growth and self-fulfillment. The primary device used by the great masses of people in this struggle for advancement and protection was the trade unions, which sought to do away with the suffering of the workers through concerted action, both economic and political.

The purchase of an individual's labor caused him to lose control over the determination of "his physical, intellectual, social, and ethical existence" (p. 100). An inability to sell his labor had even more dire consequences for the worker, who was then no longer able to support himself. The reasons for these "peculiarities" of labor included the inequality which existed between the employer and the employed and the resulting one-sidedness of the individual contract determining the laborer's wages and working conditions. Additionally, an employer's ability to exercise power over the worker created a condition of dependency reflected in the worker's health, his "mental and moral development," and the political and religious aspects of his life. Inherent in modern industrial employment is the inability of a worker to provide the economic security he seeks without organization.

But organized labor has an effect upon working-class life which far exceeds the economic aspects of a worker's existence. Trade union activity has the capacity of imparting a higher tone to the political life of the nation. The result will be greater honesty and morality in politics as the working class proves itself capable of greater and greater independent political action. Trade unions will have the effect of furthering the brotherhood of man through their various economic, political, and educational activities. "The labor movement, as the facts would indicate, is the strongest force outside the Christian Church making for the practical recognition of human brotherhood" (p. 138). The trade union's role as an instrument of mutual insurance to protect against the ravages of industrial life is another illustration of this higher calling of the labor movement.

At the base of all trade union activity is the conviction that the existent legal, economic, and social institutions are not capable of providing satisfactory living conditions for the working class; thus trade unions are used to obtain forcibly the benefits which society denies their members. Unlike the utopians, who advocated a complete transformation in organized society's rationale and structure, Ely proposed a middle ground through the use of arbitration and cooperation. He felt that cooperation did not seek or need a complete transformation of the legal basis of society, as it sought the voluntary unification of labor and capital.

Ely advocated the use of arbitration as a means of settling disputes between labor and management, and he felt that the existence of viable trade unions was an essential ingredient for making arbitration work. This power of organized labor was his answer to the problems created by the fact that human nature was "too weak to be entrusted with despotic power in an industrial system or anywhere else. Laborers will be ground into the dust if they cannot protect themselves by combination" (p. 147). Arbitration was the logical answer to the loathing which labor and management felt toward the use of the strike.

In spite of his advocacy of arbitration, however, Ely did not negate the use of the strike as a fundamental element in the relationship between organized workers and their employers. Strikes were not self-defeating in all cases; they occupied an essential role in the system of industrial governance. Ely held it as a truism that the willingness and the ability to strike could produce more favorable terms of employment than would otherwise be possible. Strikes do work; and the success of strikes in improving conditions of employment led to the use of the strike weapon as a means of forcing an employer to deal with unions representing his employees. Organizational strikes, however, were a sign of weakness on the part of trade unions which were unable to force their will upon employers by the use of other means. Ely felt it an absolute necessity to recognize the fact that labor organizations were a permanent part of the industrial and societal arena. Industrial peace would be obtained when this fact is accepted, and unions then would have achieved the recognition they seek (pp. 149–52, 162).

Cooperation, however, was the cornerstone of Ely's program for human betterment. In his discussion of distributive cooperation, he stated that such combinations of purchasers in various forms were only a partial answer to the problems raised by industrial society, for while distributive cooperation divided profits, it involved no unification of labor and capital. He viewed distributive cooperation as a training ground, a beginning which would lead to more important transformations.

> While co-operative distribution adopts as its maxim, "Competence to the purchaser," productive co-operation finds a watchword in, "Competence to the workman." The first benefits the laborer indirectly. It helps him as a consumer but not as a workingman. . . . It does not enter into the sphere of his activities as a producer. Co-operation in production, however, takes hold at one of the more vital problems of the relations between capital and labor. (p. 180)

Distributors' cooperatives precede producers' cooperatives because the latter are much more complex in nature; hence the educational role of the former. Profit sharing is an elementary form of productive cooperation, but pure productive cooperation involves the workers in decision-making procedures. The role of the employer is abolished, and the workers employ themselves. The workers are generally also the stockholders of the enterprise, and they may decide to designate a portion of the profits for a specific purpose such as education or leisure activities. While interest is paid on the capital investment, all surplus profit is paid to the workers themselves (pp. 167–81).

The device of cooperation was not limited to distribution and production. Cooperative insurance and credit schemes also existed. Ely saw cooperation as having achieved a good deal of success in the United States, and he felt it to be a vigorous and vital force in American society. Its failures resulted largely from the isolation of the workers in American industrial society, a lack of stability in the rate of employment, and the heterogeneous nature of the American population. Despite these obstacles, he painted a very optimistic picture for the future of cooperation given a favorable environment (pp. 209–11, 219).

Ely did not display the same view toward socialistic schemes which sought the overthrow of existing economic, political, and social institutions. However, he did recognize differences in method and character among the major forms of socialism that grew out of the European revolutions of 1848.

He considered the International Working People's Association to be nihilist in its political philosophy, objecting to present forms of government while seeking to replace them with political institutions of comparable authority. He had nothing but contempt for the "Internationalists" who sought the destruction of all institutions, even those of value to both society and to the individual. He felt that those who advocated societal change by violence should be controlled and constrained; but he did not confuse these anarchists with milder forms of socialists (pp. 231–42). The Socialist Labor Party, for example, differed from the anarchists both in goals and in method. Rejecting the use of violence, the SLP tended to view revolution as part of the natural course of societal evolution. As long as socialists thus restricted themselves to peaceful methods, Ely felt that there should be no abridgment of their right to speak freely. Although he did not believe that socialism offered a better form of society to the populace, he viewed peaceful socialism as seeking a "union of social factors." Since he was convinced of the need for movement in this direction, he saw the socialists as presenting no current danger.

In concluding his manuscript, Ely called for the suppression of violence. The preservation of domestic tranquility was even more important for the worker than for the employer, as violence was totally inconsistent with the maintenance of societal benefits. He also opposed the use of the boycott as a weapon against employers; he saw such activity as completely different from a quiet and peaceful appeal against a "gross abuse." He dismissed the extreme individualism of the age as immoral and called for the adoption of Christian ethics and morality as economic necessities. In addition, the number of people to whom those ethics should be applied ought to be expanded. Ely felt that enlightened employers who sided with the causes of the workers comprised a conservative element in society and could negate the need for violent and destructive action on the part of the working class.

In conclusion, Ely found four institutions in society which must be used to better the condition of the working class and, in fact, all classes: (1) the union, (2) the state, (3) the school, and, of course, (4) the church (pp. 295–324).

John R. Commons

The works of John R. Commons represent a revolt against classical economics which created models of atomized fragments of competition. Commons asserted that the key to an understanding of economic behavior was the behavior of groups, not individuals, and he believed that critical economic decisions are embodied in institutions and customs. Value is settled by conflict; it is not derived from any rationally inductive process. Commons opposed the notion of "natural rights," holding that rights come from national and other forms of collective action and therefore are not "natural."[6]

Commons's explanation of the advent of trade unionism is that it developed with the first form of capitalism, which was distributive in nature and did not coincide with the appearance of the machine and the factory system. Trade unions in the United States developed from peculiarly American conditions, and a knowledge of these conditions is essential in distinguishing between American unions and those of other countries. One important special feature of the United States was the presence and abundance of free land, which allowed the oppressed to escape from infringements on their property and political rights.[7] The vastness of the county and the "spreading network of transportation" also distinguished the American experience. The most distinctive feature of the American environment, however, was the amount of immigration and the resulting heterogeneity of the population. This created the exclusive nature of the American trade union movement.[8]

The winning of universal male suffrage long before it was achieved in other countries gave the worker a share in political decision making and created a cycle in which unions alternated between economic and political action. The restrictions on trade unions created by laws and the courts negated labor's political struggles and forced unions to seek gains through economic power developed by means of collective bargaining.

Commons traced the evolution of trade unionism back to the "craft-guild" stage of production which predated unionism. He discovered two such organizations existing in Boston in 1648, corporations of shoemakers and coopers,[9] and chose the shoemakers for his explanation of union development. The guild sought to suppress inferior workers, and it began when the itinerant shoemaker working at his home had been replaced by the shoemaker working in a shop. The guild sought to protect itself against the inferior work of the itinerant, and it substituted piecework rates for payment in goods or lodging. In the guild, the functions of the merchant, the master craftsman, and the journeymen workers were all combined in the same individual.[10]

By the end of the eighteenth century, the masters found themselves faced with two sets of problems: the competition of cheaper grades of products sold in the public marketplace and a comparable form of competition from masters who advertised goods at lower prices. This caused the organization of a society of masters to protect their function as merchants. This development was caused not by the introduction of new technology but by the presence of new markets. The result of these events was the end of the craft-guild stage of production and the beginning of the retail-shop stage. In addition to custom-order or "bespoke work," the journeymen shoemakers now produced shop work for the open market. The individual who now performed the functions of both master and merchant assembled "a stock of shoes made in dull times at low wages, and instead of a price-bargain made *before* the work is done, as in the custom-order stage, it is made *after* the work is done."[11] This required a capital investment in raw material, finished goods, and individual credit, and it often involved providing journeymen with raw material to be worked on at their homes and returned to the shop.

This marked the beginning of the separation of the master's interests from those of the journeymen, but only the beginning. With the improvement of transportation through the introduction of pikes and canals at the end of the eighteenth century, the new master-merchants sought retailers in distant markets. Thus the individual who combined the functions of both master and merchant took on a new function—that of wholesaler. This marked the wholesale-order stage of production in the shoemaking industry. The journeyman now found himself making goods for three different markets and facing three different types of competition: in addition to producing goods for the retail markets, he was also producing products for a larger wholesale market while keeping up production of goods for the older custom-order market.

The expansion of the market to the wholesale-order stage brought added expenses to the master-merchant in the forms of transportation and the acquisition of new business. As no change in the methods of production accompanied the widening of the marketplace, outside competition could be met and the quality of goods maintained only through the reduction of wages. This caused the journeymen to organize to preserve and guarantee wage rates and exclude scabs from the production of shoes. In defense, the employers organized to prevent such activities. The result was the conspiracy cases of the early nineteenth century, in which the journeymen were found guilty of conspiring to injure nonmembers of their society and to injure the public through higher prices.[12]

This marked the complete separation of master-merchant and journeyman and initiated the first permanent wage-earning class in American society. The wage bargain assumed extreme importance as the merchant was under pressure to reduce the wages of the journeymen. The conflict between labor and capital had begun, and with it the first trade unions.

At the next stage of production (about 1835), the merchant-capitalist entered the scene. This individual had not worked his way up from apprentice to journeyman to master, and may not have had any knowledge of the technology by which the finished products were produced. His sole function was that of a merchant. The raw materials used in production were owned by the merchant-capitalist, and the market became speculative.

In the merchant-capitalist stage of production, the small employers became master-workmen and labor contractors, competing against each other. They also found themselves in competition with the other forms of production available to the merchant-capitalist, including convict labor and home production.

The end result of the competitive pressure on the small contractor was the sweatshop with its downward pressure on wages. This increased the conflict between labor and capital, which was intensified by the additional advantages open to the merchant-capitalist. First removing the wholesale-order business from the retail merchant, he forced this merchant from his function as employer. Without the necessary capital, the former master-merchant became a labor contractor, a specialist in wage bargaining. Financial capital took the place of technological capital, and the merchant-capitalist was in a position to make use of bank credit. He took over the wholesale business, and the wholesale-speculative stage of production emerged.[13] The constantly widening market initiated by these stages of production removed the journeyman ever farther from the market in which his goods were sold.

The final stage in this evolution of the production process involved the introduction of machines, and the small contractor now became a manufacturer. The cycle was completed with the former journeyman losing the tools of production which he had formerly owned. Note that this stage of production was the first to involve a change in the tools of production; all the previous stages took place without the introduction of the factory system. The shift to mechanization created marginal producers who acted as a competitive menace, and caused the introduction of unskilled workers or "green hands" to work the new machines.

The necessity for organizations to protect workers was brought about by the changes in the structure of the market which caused a divergence of interest between the master-merchant and the journeyman. Earlier organizations established for protection against inferior goods yielded to organizations of journeymen designed to protect the financial side of the bargain between the employer and the society. This marked the loss of control over quality on the part of the journeymen. The introduction of the machine introduced a new type of organizational goal.[14]

The formation of the Knights of St. Crispin in 1868 signaled this change. The organization's actions centered around two issues: the reduction of wages and the use of "green hands." Since the factory produced goods which were equal or superior in quality to those produced by the journeymen, this new protest was designed to save the craft. Thus the Knights severely restricted instruction in the craft to new individuals.[15]

The Knights' actions led to the establishment of working rules surrounding the trade. This development certainly was not restricted to the shoemakers; it was a major technique by which unions sought to protect themselves against both employers and the machine. Such rules grew out of the settlement of disputes, and could be offensive or defensive in nature. They comprised the "collective will" of the organization, bringing the power of the group to bear upon the individual. Being designed to unify a mass of workers, they constitute a social process.[16] (Compare the Webbs' notion of a common rule, discussed later in this chapter.)

Frank Tannenbaum[17]

Frank Tannenbaum's thinking about trade unions was altered during the thirty years between the publication of his two major treatises on the subject. He first dealt with the change in society caused by various social phenomena, including the changes in the methods of manufacturing goods. Every change has a multiplier effect, causing alterations in other facets of human existence, and a basic correlative of change is insecurity. Thus the immediate effects of the machine age are the undesirable ones of uncertainty and powerlessness. The powers which control the relationship between an individual and his job are beyond the control of that individual, and the threat of unemployment is constant. Insecurity permeates all social relationships to so great an extent that it is the major source of conflict in society. "Insecurity is the dominant fact in the lives of every class in the community; no one escapes it" (*LM*, p. 5).

The major characteristic of industrial society, and also the major cause of insecurity, is the use of the machine. Every factory involves not only an assemblage of machinery, but also a large and complicated grouping of human beings who perform jobs demanded of them by the machine process. The relationship to the machine becomes the central focus of a worker's life and the new "center of gravity" or commonality of interest for the working class. Whereas the former basis of community organization was the land or commerce, the basis of organized society is restructured by the use of the machine, and the control of the machine and its use is the major single problem which faces the labor movement.

The organization of the labor movement is thus an exercise in self-defense—an attempt to establish some stability amidst the insecurity and uncertainty caused by the machine. "Unless we see the labor movement as an irresistible coming together of men in terms of the tools and the industry which they use in common, for the purposes of greater security by more effective control of them, we cannot and do not understand the labor movement at all" (*LM*, p. 31). In this joining together to do battle against the competition engendered by the capitalistic system, workers create a form of organization with repercussions far exceeding the original purpose of the labor movement. Likewise, organization according to craft or industry provides a degree of security far exceeding that which an individual can obtain on his own. For the worker, the labor movement becomes the means to maintain stability in a changing, dynamic world.

In this struggle against the owners of the machines, the labor movement has allies among other elements of society who seek stability and security. The effect of this organization upon the employing enterprise is fundamental and unavoidable. The greater the power which labor organizations possess, the greater are the number of restrictions placed upon employers. The struggle between the security-conscious worker and the employer seeking to avoid restrictions on his actions is inevitable, and it apparently must continue until one of the two interest groups succeeds in forcing its will upon the other.

> There are apparently only two possible alternatives. Either the business community is going to destroy the labor movement or the labor movement will absorb the control and power now in the hands of the business community and by such absorption displace competition and substitute cooperation. The . . . method of organized labor . . . seems to predicate the displacement of the capitalist system by industrial democracy. . . . (LM, p. 44)

The instability which the use of the machine creates portends constant friction and change for society as a whole. The initial impetus for this comes from the total loathing which workers feel for the dehumanizing effects of the machine, a hatred which is soothed by the organization of trade unions. The labor movement is also born of conscious struggle, and the resulting "class consciousness" reflects the notion that the ill effects accompanying the use of the machine are preventable given a collective volition to alter the situation.

Organized labor seeks to replace the despair of unorganized group consciousness with constructive change requiring as little conflict as is possible. Lack of organization, and employer opposition to organization, lend themselves to a destructive form of unorganized power—"the power of the mob." Unlike unions, which organize this discontent, socialism delays actions intended to alleviate the problems which workers face. Socialism "concerns itself about those problems *rather than with them*" (*LM*, p. 65), and distracts the attention of the workers from the forces immediate to the insecurity which they face.

The capacity for creativity within the labor movement helps to differentiate it from socialism and other political movements. Through labor organization a worker is able to find the constructive alternatives to machine-produced helplessness, insecurity, and despair. Thus it, not the socialist party, is a real force for social change and by definition revolutionary in nature (*LM*, pp. 52–66, 70–71).

The labor movement seeks to replace governance by a small part of the community and to make the running of industry a group function. This quest for industrial democracy represents the movement's nonmaterial goals. In seeking this dignity and responsibility, the worker makes the union "the center of his emotional outlet as well as the center of his social connections. This process is in part a transmutation of the material into the spiritual" (*LM*, p. 96). This educational function of the union movement makes it the "people's university."

Tannenbaum uses the word "comradeship" to describe this spirit which unions generate, and he claims that the spiritual and social changes created by unions make them revolutionary in character. Through union membership, individuals come to treasure their "labor and not their possessions" (*LM*, p. 111). Thus all of organized labor is in fact revolutionary because it involves the social transformation of its membership. A union embodies a change even if that change is not entirely completed. This marks the basic difference between a union and a political party: while a political party may be either radical or conservative, a union is incapable of maintaining the *status quo*. Even a reformist or radical political party cannot accomplish what a labor union in fact does, for a union embodies a realignment of the forces prevailing in a society. While a political party needs to achieve power which can be used indirectly after it is organized, a union achieves power which can be applied directly after organization.

The struggle for organization is the major fight which a union faces, and power follows this struggle. "Labor is thus revolutionary, not because it organizes for purposes of control and change, but because its very organization is the essence of control and change" (*LM*, p. 118). All unions, whether their program be conservative or radical, possess the inevitable effect of ending capitalism by taking control from the hands of the capitalist and placing it in the hands of the workers. To the conservative trade unionist, this is a consequence; to the revolutionary trade unionist it is both a consequence and an ideal.

The labor movement is able to eliminate competition because of its membership's community of social and economic interest. In so doing, it makes revolutions unnecessary in the long run. This is what gives the labor movement its conservative function: it "transmutes economic interests to spiritual values and makes progress pragmatic rather than violently revolutionary" (*LM*, p. 175).

In *A Philosophy of Labor*, Tannenbaum loses his preoccupation with the revolutionary nature of labor unions. Instead he comes to view them as conservative and counterrevolutionary. He again cites the common interest in work itself as the basis of a union's strength, but he claims that it is able to accomplish its ends without pursuing any utopia. Noting once more the insecurity created by the use of the machine, Tannenbaum sees the production of a permanent wage-earning class. Trade unionism is seen as being counterrevolutionary because it has sought to reestablish the values of justice, security, and dignity lost through the industrial revolution without a definite ideology or sense of direction. Its conservatism lies in its creative nature and its capacity to build step by step. In recognizing the commonality of interest which work creates, unions have survived by filling the void in social and moral status caused by industrial change (*PL*, pp. 3–13, 32–71).

The wage system created by the industrial revolution destroyed the status system which had previously existed, and the factory system became predominant. This created workers with a commonality of interest based on their employment and matters related to it. A new society created a new sense of identity. Unions developed spontaneously at the local level, and survived in the long run because they fulfilled the new needs of workers.

The utopians considered the trade unions either as useless because they were unable to accomplish any real societal change (the socialists) or as interferences in the free market (the classical economists). Nevertheless, the unionists succeeded where the utopians failed. Similarly, the revolutionaries viewed collective bargaining with management as class betrayal, and sought to abolish the existing social order rather than recognize an inherent difference of interest between the managers and the managed. The unions thus needed an educator to guide them under the broader program of the party instead of the narrower functions of trade unions. It is natural "that the commitment (of the revolutionary) to a universal design should make him contemptuous of trade-unionism as something of no major significance unless he could bend it to his own broad ends" (PL, p. 95). The ends were more important than the means to the revolutionary; the ends and means of the unionist, however, were more immediate and tangible. Trade unionists devoted to improving conditions on the job became "business-minded" and less controllable by the revolutionary. There is a definite correlation between the degree of industrial development and the lack of control of the party over the union. Unions, in fact, represent a structural alteration within a nation's economy.

> The trade-union is not a reform movement; it is not a political party; it is not revolutionary in intent; it is not a legislative activity. It may at times contribute to all of these, but it is none of them. It is the formal expression of the socially inevitable grouping of men in modern industry. . . . (PL, p. 106)

The rights and privileges of workers are embodied in the collective agreement, which is a means for dealing with the inevitable conflict between order giver and order taker. Both sides subscribe to the mutually developed system of rules. While it does not rest on some unique principle, the agreement builds upon precedent in seeking to meet the needs and expectations of the workers. The union fills the gap in moral status created by the industrial revolution by means of the collective agreement, and in so doing it secures the loyalty of its membership which is necessary for survival. The agreement is an ideal tool for dealing with the disputes which arise as the union makes inroads upon the prerogatives of the employer, and it recognizes that an agreement reached "on one contentious issue merely raises another" (PL, p. 165). Tannenbaum thus changed his view of unions as inherently revolutionary organizations to unions as devices seeking to meet their members' needs and aspirations through the institutionalization of conflict.

Robert F. Hoxie[18]

Robert F. Hoxie divided his study of trade unionism into the two basic areas of structure and function. He felt that the environment, particularly the economic environment, was the chief force underlying the creation of unionism, and that the development of trade unionism was a reaction or a series of adaptations to changes in the environment in which workers existed. In his view, a study of the history of trade unionism

> reveals the fact that unionism has not a single genesis, but that it has made its appearance time after time, independently, wherever in the modern era a group of workers, large or small, has developed a strong internal consciousness of common interests. (p. 34)

Such a study further reveals that unions undergo a constant series of changes both structurally and functionally, as responses to alterations in the problems which workers face. This affirmation of union opportunism supports the statement that "unionists have been prone to act first and to formulate theories afterward" (p. 34).

The key to Hoxie's explanation of the phenomenon of trade unionism lies in his notion of distinct union types, both structurally and functionally. He distinguishes four basic union structural types: (1) the craft union, (2) the crafts or trades union, (3) the industrial union, and (4) the labor union. Craft unions are organized around a specific occupation or skill, and consist of a national union which unites a series of local unions into a single entity. The crafts or trades union differs from the craft union in that it is a federation of unions found in differing occupations or industries. It is structured into local, state, and national segments, and is organized geographically (unlike the craft union, which is organized around a job or industry).

The industrial union is organized according to the specific industry in which its members are employed. It includes within its membership both skilled and unskilled workers producing the same or substantially the same product or products. Its scope of organization has the same boundaries as the firms which it organizes, and it is based on local unions differentiated according to geographical districts. At the top of this type of structure is the national union. The fourth type, the labor union, might also be called a general union, since it seeks to organize all workers geographically regardless of their skill or industry.

Hoxie also identified two structural types which do not fit into any of the above four categories. The first of these he called the compound craft or crafts union. The basic difference between this and a craft union is that a compound craft union organizes workers who are not employed in the same occupation and is not based upon workers employed in a single industry. It rather consists of a consolidation of workers performing different skilled jobs. Finally, the quasi industrial federation is composed of both craft and compound craft unions. These constituent unions retain their own identity and sovereignty but join together to protect their common interests (pp. 37–44, 55–57, 355–57).

Hoxie maintained that unions must be studied according to their function as well as their structure; but the structural form which unionism assumes is based upon its function. Hoxie assumes that the union is an expression of group psychology. It thus gets its functional characteristics from a combination of environmental conditions and the individual needs and characteristics of its membership. Evolving by a trial-and-error method, the "problems and conditions" which a union faces determine its function, and once this occurs, its "function determines structure" (p. 99).

Trade union members comprise a functional social group. "A functional social group may be defined as a body of individuals holding a common viewpoint in regard to one or a number of vital social matters and at this respect at variance with the viewpoints of other members of society" (p. 355). This common interest in issues that relate to matters of common concern may be either broad or narrow. Though individual union members may be divided on many issues, they are united on issues relating to their occupation, and this like-mindedness tends to draw them together. Unionism is thus an illustration of individuals with similar temperaments, facing comparable environments and having mutual interests to band together as a group for common action (pp. 354–59).

As a natural reaction to the forces which shape their working and nonworking lives, workers develop a social outlook—a set of beliefs concerning how their condition can be bettered. A group consciousness develops surrounding the common interests in improvements at the work site and in society, and unions are formed to seek these betterments through a variety of means. Workers thus form unions not to establish a particular type of organization "but to establish and maintain certain conditions of living—to put through a remedial program based on their common interpretation of the social situation viewed from the standpoint of their immediate conditions and needs (p. 59).

Hoxie distinguished four functional varieties of trade union: (1) business unionism, (2) friendly or uplift unionism, (3) revolutionary unionism, and (4) predatory unionism. Business unionism is most characteristically the philosophy of craft and compound craft structural types. It is job conscious rather than class conscious, expressing the concerns of those workers in a specific skill. Disregarding utopian schemes, business unionism seeks immediate gains, and it seeks these gains for its membership rather than for the working class or society as a whole. Thus it is exclusive rather than inclusive in nature. Its philosophy may be called conservative, since it accepts as inevitable the existence of capitalism, and the wage system. The method by which it seeks to maintain and improve the condition of its membership is collective bargaining, and it scorns political action. It tends to develop a strong internal government with a strong leadership, although the members will vote a leader out of office if he fails in his primary function of craft protection and betterment.

In vivid contrast, friendly or uplift unionism is idealistic and utopian in its philosophy. While friendly unionism is essentially peaceful and law-abiding, it tends to think in terms of the interests of the working class or society as a whole. In addition to improving an employee's working conditions, uplift unionism seeks to improve the moral, intellectual, and cultural life of the worker and to protect him against the ravages of disease, unemployment, and old age. While it may use collective bargaining as a tool, uplift unionism advocates larger political programs to elevate the status of the worker.

The third type, revolutionary unionism, is neither peaceful nor law-abiding. It is strongly class-conscious rather than job-conscious, sees a basic disharmony of interest between the employing class and the employed, and accepts neither the system of private ownership nor the wage system. It views as useless the collective bargaining of business unionism and the mutual assistance programs of uplift unionism. Its radical activities coincide with its radical ideology.

Revolutionary unions are of two types. The first views as both necessary and harmonious the amalgamation of the trade unions and the socialist parties. Its ultimate goal is the socialist society, and its means of obtaining this goal is political action of a class nature. The second type of revolutionary unionism repudiates collective bargaining as class collaboration and views both political action and socialism as being worthless and oppressive. It advocates direct action through industrial sabotage and seeks a society based on an industrial association of workers. This functional type of trade unionism was best illustrated by the Industrial Workers of the World.

By contrast, predatory unionism is totally pragmatic in nature. It will use any of the three previously mentioned methods to achieve its immediate ends, and it will seek these goals ruthlessly.

As is the case with revolutionary unionism, there are two distinct types of predatory unions. The first, hold-up unionism, usually is to be found in the disguise of business unionism. It operates through collective bargaining with no principles guiding its actions, and it is both boss-ridden and corrupt. The leaders of hold-up unions frequently join with employers to monopolize the labor and management sides of the employment relationship to the detriment of the union members and the public. Rival unions and rival employers are not tolerated. Guerrilla unionism, the second type of predatory unionism, also operates without fixed principles and will use any means to achieve its ends, but it always exists in opposition to employers, never in collusion with them. It adopts violent methods because it despairs of achieving its ends through legitimate means (pp. 44–51).

The Webbs[19]

Sidney and Beatrice Webb were members of the influential Fabian Society in Great Britain. The society derived its name from Quintus Fabius Maximus, the Roman general who defeated the armies of Carthage under the command of Hannibal by avoiding battle unless it was on his own terms. His name, and that of the Fabians, became synonymous with a policy of gradualism.

The Webbs dealt with the origins of trade unionism in *The History of Trade Unionism,* written just before the turn of the century. They defined a trade union as "a continuous association of wage-earners for the purpose of maintaining or improving the conditions of their working lives" (*HTU,* p. 1).

Trade unions, according to the Webbs, did not evolve from the old craft guilds. The authority and functions of the medieval guilds rested upon the presence within their ranks of the real directors of production, and the master craftsman was the central figure in their operation. They were not created out of any hostility to authority, but rather served a policing function that guaranteed the quality of finished products. The guilds represented a number of interests in the production process, and the guild member cannot be defined as an employee in the commonly accepted definition of that term.

The rise of trade unions occurred in the era following that of the guild system, as a result of the economic revolution which accompanied the industrial revolution in England. In every instance, unions came into being when the majority of workers had lost their independence as producers of finished products and had become permanent wage earners. Since the establishment of a business enterprise required more capital than a journeyman could accumulate within a limited number of years, a divorce occurred between labor and capital—between the direction of enterprise and the execution of these directions. This trend was irreversible given the realities of the industrial revolution.

The differentiation between labor and capital (and their respective functions) was accelerated by the ever-increasing necessity to accumulate more capital resources once the initiation of the factory system had begun. The system fed upon itself, and success called for more capital development. In some cases, the high price of both raw materials and tools or machines further added to this divorce of labor from capital. While it is easy to understand how the massing of workers under the factory roof gave rise to the development of trade unions, in some instances this phenomenon was caused merely by the separation of the functions of the capitalist entrepreneur and the manual laborer.

The Webbs did not assume a correlation between the development of this permanent wage-earning class and the use of the machine in production. The introduction of the machine and the use of power led to the factory system, but the first trade unions did not appear with the advent of the factory; they preceded this development. The earliest combinations of workers to pursue their own interests occurred when production was performed by hand, nearly a century before the appearance of the factory system and the use of machinery (*HTU*, pp. 25–26).

By 1842, notions of social revolution had been largely set aside by English trade unionists. Instead, they organized themselves to overcome the harshest of the legal devices used to suppress them, and to ease the industrial oppression from which they suffered. Years of economic prosperity coincided with the improved financial status of trade unions and a greater permanence on the part of their membership. As the unions developed the strength to resist legal oppression, the benefits of united action became clearly visible. Trade unions with moderate aims succeeded where those of the revolutionary period of 1829–1842 had failed (*HTU*, pp. 31–41, 180–87).

The years 1889 and 1890 saw the development of the "new unionism" in which trade union activity assumed a new aggressiveness as its leaders sought to bring within their ranks the great mass of unorganized unskilled workers. "They aimed, not at superseding existing social structures, but at capturing them all in the interests of the wage-earners" (*HTU*, pp. 377, 414–25). The new unionists saw themselves as living in a democratic social structure, impossible to destroy and foolish to ignore. The mentality of the trade union movement had widened to include the broadest possible range of workers, and they found willing political allies from outside the trade unions themselves. This was largely the result of the acceptance of the fact that the division of labor and capital was no passing phase, but was becoming more rigidly entrenched as the industrial revolution evolved.

In addition to examining the origins of trade unions, the Webbs dealt extensively with their functioning. The old and the new unions were found to act in a similar manner (*ID*, pp. 146–47), using three methods to enforce their regulations: (1) mutual insurance, (2) collective bargaining, and (3) legal enactment.

The method of mutual insurance involves the various internal trade union or "friendly society" benefits: sick pay, accident benefits, burial money, and payments to members when they are unemployed. Although the purpose of these benefits is to provide protection and maintenance when a union member is deprived of his or her livelihood, the trade union itself derives several advantages from supplying them. The major gain to the union is that the benefits tend to bind the membership together and to attract new members. In addition, as the contributions made to support these benefits are placed into a general fund, the union establishes a financial reserve which can be used in time of organizational need. The practice also provides for a form of control over the union's members; loss of benefits upon voluntarily leaving or being expelled from the union is a penalty that aids in imposing and reinforcing trade union discipline.

Protecting members who are out of work is a humane reaction to the failure of existing legislation to provide for this support. This benefit also permits a member to refuse work which pays less than the going rate and allows the union to forbid the acceptance of such employment. This was seen by the Webbs as a method by which a union may enforce a "common rule"—"the enforcement of a minimum, below which no employer may descend, never a maximum, beyond which he may not, if he chooses, offer better terms" (ID, p. 715). That is, the union may ensure without striking that a given rate is paid on a job. If an employer finds that he is unable to obtain or retain workers at a substandard wage, the pressure of the resulting instability will force him to meet the going rate (ID, pp. 150–72).

The method of collective bargaining involves several workers dealing with an employer on behalf of the larger group to establish a common rule, that is, minimum and standardized rates of pay. It is a substitute for the individual bargain between an employee and his employer. Development of the machinery for collective bargaining coincided with the growth of the scale of industry. It is an art or skill which is not left to the rank-and-file union member, but calls for a trained union negotiator. Once a common rule is established through the mechanism of collective bargaining with an employer, it is extended throughout the enterprise. The method of collective bargaining thus directly concerns the job-related interests of the membership (ID, pp. 173–221).

The third method attributed by the Webbs to trade unions was that of legal enactment, in which unions seek their ends through a political program resulting in parliamentary action. The increased participation of workers in the political life of a country results in a more extensive use of this method. Resorting to the law is a slower process than collective bargaining, but its difficulty does not dissuade unions from its use. An act of parliament forces unanimity; therefore, "however tedious and difficult may be the process of obtaining it, once the Common Rule is embodied in an Act of Parliament, it satisfies more perfectly the Trade Union aspirations of permanence and universality than any other method" (ID, p. 255). This method also is logical in situations in which the trade unions are part of a three-pronged labor movement also consisting of a cooperative movement and a labor or socialist party (*ID*, pp. 247–78).

Political action is a way of extending the benefits gained through collective bargaining to workers who do not enjoy the benefits of this relationship with their employers. Such activity has both selfish and altruistic purposes behind it: It is a way of protecting the common rule established by negotiations, and at the same time fulfills the social consciousness of unions that feel a sense of responsibility to the unorganized.

The Webbs were also concerned with the status of the individual worker facing the "higgling of the market," and they felt that the essential economic weakness of the individual worker was well known to management. Thus, union economic activities involved the restriction of numbers as well as the use of the common rule.

The Webbs were the first theorists to view trade unions as no less relevant under socialism than under capitalism. They claimed that all managers of industry, whether they be in the private sector or "appointed by the consumers or citizens" (*ID*, p. 819), have a vested interest in producing goods or providing services at the cheapest possible cost. "It follows . . . that Trade Unionism is not merely an incident of the present phase of capitalist industry, but has a permanent function to fulfill in the democratic state" (*ID*, p. 823). Even under greater public control of industry, where a decision to nationalize is based on a much broader range of issues than the interests of organized union employees, unions will still play an essential role in a democracy. This role involves both a narrow program of collective bargaining and a larger political program which marshals the bulk of union members.

Marx and Lenin[20]

Marxism is often said to be a form of secular religion, as it consists of both a comprehensive theory of the world and a program of action. Marx's materialistic interpretation of history, historical materialism, portrays an uncontrollable economic development of history which is marked by revolutions leading to successive historical stages. Economic development must pass through specific stages referred to as a dialectic process.

According to Marx, societal history "is the history of class struggles," and society is dividing itself into two hostile classes—the bourgeoisie and the proletariat (*CM*, pp. 9–10). The bourgeoisie has played its own revolutionary role in societal development by destroying preexisting feudal conditions, and by establishing monetary relationships in place of those based on natural superiority.

The modern worker is able to exist only because he is able to find work, and this situation lasts only as long as his work increases the amount of capital. As its use grows, machinery depresses wages, and workers band together to fight this downward pressure on wages. Only by abolishing the capitalist system can workers end these conditions. To do so requires political supremacy which surpasses national boundaries and imposes the centralized control of production by the state (*CM*, pp. 12–21, 29–31). "The immediate aim of the Communists is the same as that of all the other proletarian parties: Formation of the proletariat into a class, overthrow of bourgeois supremacy, conquest of political power by the proletariat" (*CM*, p. 23). This requires the abolition of private property.

For Marx, the study of capitalist economies begins with commodities. Each commodity has use value; that is, it must be useful and not merely produced for the marketplace. However, use value alone does not make an object a commodity; it must also have exchange value, which is created because human labor alone is capable of creating market value. According to the labor theory of value, the amount of value embodied in a commodity is determined by the amount of labor, measured by time—the socially necessary labor time—used in its production (*C*, pp. 41–45). "The labour-time socially necessary is that required to produce an article under the normal conditions of production, and with the average degree of skill and intensity prevalent at the time" (*C*, p. 46).

The value of labor as a commodity is determined by the value of the "means of subsistence" required to maintain the worker. The labor used in the production of a product must constantly be replaced by new labor. Subsistence is thus measured in terms of the amount needed to allow a worker to provide for replacements "by procreation." But the value that a worker adds to a product is greater than the value of that worker's subsistence. This difference is the surplus value of a commodity which is "appropriated" by the capitalist. If an amount of labor less than the time a worker actually puts in on a job is all that is needed to provide for subsistence, this does not keep him from working for a full day. "Therefore, the value of labour-power, and the value which that labour-power creates in the labour process, are two entirely different magnitudes; and this difference of the two values was what the capitalist had in view, when he was purchasing the labour-power" (*C*, pp. 215–16). The key for the employer is that labor is capable of producing an amount of value which is greater than itself.

The means of production can add value to a finished product only equal to themselves. Since the portion of capital comprised of the means of production does not "undergo any quantitative alteration of value," Marx calls it constant capital. Unlike constant capital, that comprised of labor is capable of an alteration of value; that is, of producing an amount of surplus value. This is designated as variable capital. Thus the function of machinery is to decrease the amount of variable capital, thereby producing more surplus value. In the long run, a tendency exists for the capitalist to use an increasing amount of machinery to increase the proportion of constant capital—to alter the organic composition of capital. As this proportion changes, the demand for variable capital decreases at an ever-accelerating rate.

The expected result of the decreased demand for variable (human) capital is increased unemployment, and the development of a "reserve army" of unemployed is subject to cyclical changes which are a necessary part of capitalist systems of production.

But this drive for the increased mechanization of production leading to more surplus value and exploitation causes the amount of constant capital to increase at a greater rate than the rate of exploitation. Since variable capital is the only form of capital capable of producing value greater than itself, the use of increased proportions of constant capital leads to decreasing levels of profit. The capitalist is forced into this contradictory situation by the intensity of competition. As the rate of profit is driven to lower and lower levels, the competitive pressure increases, and the number of employers decreases. As capital is concentrated in fewer individuals, the "misery" of the working class increases. This immiseration is a historical necessity; it is the result of the decreased demand for labor as the use and proportion of constant capital increases (*C*, pp.

232–33, 405, 690, 693, 701, 708–9). "Accumulation of wealth at one pole is, therefore, at the same time accumulation of misery, agony of toil, slavery, ignorance, brutality, mental degradation, at the opposite pole" (*C*, p. 709).

This leads to the final crisis. The tendency toward the centralization of capital causes one capitalist to destroy others on an international scale. The increased oppression of the workers which accompanies this development results in a revolt of the working class, which is always increasing in numbers, unity, and discipline.

> Centralisation of the means of production and socialisation of labour at last reach a point where they become incompatible with their capitalist integument. This integument is burst asunder. The knell of capitalist private property sounds. The expropriators are expropriated. (*C*, p. 837)

Thus capitalism collapses as a result of its inner contradictions and the ever-increasing class consciousness of the workers.

Marx's attitude toward trade unions grows naturally from his analysis of the effect of capitalism on the worker. Under the system of private property, a worker confers upon a stranger (the capitalist) an activity which the latter does not own. As labor is coerced, it does not provide for the satisfaction of any need on the part of the laborer, and the end result of his labor, the product, becomes something alien to him. Ultimately, life itself becomes hostile and alien—a mere means for the satisfaction of a need. A worker estranged from his labor is also torn away from his existence as a member of the species.

Private property and the wage system exist hand in hand and are equated with one another (*EPM*, pp. 108–17). "*An enforced increase of wages* . . . would therefore be nothing but *better payment for the slave*, and would not win either for the worker or for labor their human status and dignity" (*EPM*, pp. 117–18). Marx thus despaired of the effects that reforms could accomplish. Nothing could cause a deviation from his dialectic, and in fact, reforms would only delay the inevitable. Economic organizations of workers could accomplish nothing on their own.

Lenin deviated from Marx's notion of the usefulness of unions. He emphasized the necessity of education as a means of bringing the workers to understand their political oppression. Once this is done, the economic struggle of the workers gives them a keen awareness of the government's role in their life. While intellectuals may attempt to give the economic struggle a political character, they can never develop a political consciousness equal to that of the workers themselves. By gaining knowledge of the workers' experience in the factories, they can, however, help them to acquire the necessary political consciousness from without.

The vanguard must act to educate the workers politically and lead them toward revolution, utilizing all manifestations of discontent. Otherwise, the struggle is impossible. "The spontaneous labour movement is able by itself to create (and inevitably will create) only trade unionism, and working-class trade-union politics are precisely working-class bourgeois politics" (WD, p. 90). It is the duty of the intellectual vanguard to prevent this. They must guide the economic struggle of the workers "and bring into our camp increasing numbers of the proletariat!" (WD, pp. 76–86).

3

Modern Theorists
and Model Builders

Since the advent of industrialization, endeavors have been made to develop an understanding of trade union behavior in modern societies which postdate the industrial revolution. Some of these have been direct efforts to explain the phenomenon of trade unionism. Others have dealt with unions in a more indirect manner, marginal to their primary assertions. Nonetheless, they all focus upon a new role for unionism.

Richard A. Lester is directly concerned with the process of trade union evolution in describing both past developments and future trends. Mark van de Vall concerns himself with the new role which he sees unions playing in a welfare state, and rejects as anachronistic the notion of unions as organizations that merely react to their environment. The authors of *Industrialism and Industrial Man* concentrate their efforts on a description of the universality of the industrialization process and predict a new form of worker organization differing in both structure and function from those initially created by the industrial revolution.

A pair of Canadian sociologists, William A. and Margaret W. Westley, predict new problems for trade unionism in industrialized countries because of the labor force's increased education and affluence. Dealing solely with the issue of affluence and its effect on workers' industrial and political behavior, however, four British sociologists find that it plays a minimal and insignificant role.

Although he writes specifically about Indian trade unions, Fred C. Munson develops a definition of trade union structure and function which is relevant for both industrial and postindustrial society. *Strategy for Labor* represents the attempt of a French Marxist, Andre Gorz, to update Marxist ideology in the light of recent societal developments. Dual labor market theory deals with both industrial and postindustrial society and views trade union behavior in light of the development of a new conception of the labor market's functioning. The theory also predicts the source of a "new" union movement.

Daniel Bell deals specifically with trade unions in postindustrial society. Bell, a sociologist, believes that the role of organized labor in societies is based on the control of knowledge, not capital.

Richard A. Lester[1]

In *As Unions Mature*, Richard A. Lester provides a developmental theory of trade unionism. In contrast to static theories such as Perlman's and historical treatment such as Tannenbaum's, Lester creates "a systematic analysis of the institutional development of American unionism carried up to the present and projected into the future" (p. 5). In his analysis, he treats unions as devices for channeling worker protest. These protest organizations are politically oriented, both internally and externally. Internally, a union has a politically oriented leadership which establishes a machine founded on whatever patronage is available. In modern society, a union builds its power position through the use of politics, not economics. This is an understandable result of the legislative structuring of labor-management relations which has occurred in the United States. Initially using established political mechanisms to win bargaining rights, trade unions and their leadership continue to act as political organizations competing both with rival unions and with management.

In representing its members' interests, a union exists as a conflict organization seeking to institutionalize worker protest. To understand trade unions one must accept the fact that a fundamental difference in "social philosophy" exists between those who give the orders and those who take them (pp. 14, 20). The channeling of worker protest into orderly mechanisms exerts a stabilizing and constructive influence on a democratic society.

All organizations, including unions, undergo changes in structure and function as a natural corollary of their development. American unions have passed through three basic internal changes in their organizational evolution: (1) increased centralization of function and control to the national executive, (2) an increase in the status and broadening of the outlook of the national union leaders, and (3) a decrease in militancy accompanied by an increase in discipline.

With the institutionalization of collective bargaining as part of the industrial scene, there has been a shift in the focus of union functions from organizing the unorganized to the centralized administration of established collective bargaining agreements. The scope of union activities has shifted from the local level to the entire organization, and this has been accompanied by an increase in the power of the national executive. Union leaders have become administrators, and local unions have lost their status as independent sources of influence.

As this centralization develops, an alteration takes place in the top leadership of the organization. As unions are assimilated into society, the leadership function changes from one of agitation to one of skillful political administration. The scope of activities in which the union engages increases, and this widens the "interests and perspectives" of the union leadership. A balance is struck between these broader functions and representing the interests of the membership (which is vital for reelection).

While the initiation and maintenance of aggressive action such as a strike or the raising of excessive grievances brings back visions of the early, militant stages of union development, gains made through collective bargaining and the corresponding establishment of trade union rights tend to decrease the "core of conflict." Although union organizational activities tend to breed aggressiveness, the reduction in these efforts on the part of many established unions marks an absence of a source of militancy. The institutionalization of labor-management conflict through the mechanisms of negotiations and a working grievance procedure further adds to this trend (pp. 21–34).

In spite of these three tendencies, dynamic forces continue to exist in American trade unions. While a search for societal change tends to accompany the missionary spirit of early union organization, remnants of the drive for change going beyond economic issues continue to exist in some unions. Political competition may be constructive or destructive for a union, and economic competition between union and non-union workers may also play either role. Internal political rivalry tends to be more productive of dynamism than economic rivalry from without, and adverse government action may also serve as a source of invigoration. It would appear that a decrease in the challenges to union organizations and union hierarchies leads to a decrease in ideological zeal.

The very success of collective bargaining has also added to decreased dynamism in the American labor movement. Greater gains have been won through collective bargaining than through agitating for the passage of legislation, and evidence indicates that the opportunity for innovation is not as great when using economic means as when political programs are pursued. Past union achievements won through collective bargaining may have decreased the "number of new outlets" that can be broached in the scope of bargaining. "In other words, past union conquests may have curtailed the possibilities for future pioneering—at least by means of collective bargaining" (p. 56).

With the transition of the labor movement from its early organizational stage to one of "maturity," the zeal and ideals of that earlier period are eroded. The improvements which have been won in workers' standard of living and the acceptance of the achievement of economic gains as a legitimate end have reinforced this trend. There has been a corresponding decline in the degree of union democracy. Democratic controls are more effective at the local level, and with the transference of internal power upward, control of a union is more likely to resemble a political machine. Added to this is the belief that factionalization leads to collective weakness in facing employers and the government. It is pure speculation whether the present corrupting influences in American trade unionism will be reinforced by these factors; doubtless a weakening of membership control enhances the use of power for corrupt purposes (pp. 61–72).

Lester states that the history of trade union evolution is too varied to be easily differentiated according to specific stages. Instead, he distinguishes between internal and external processes of union development and between long-run tendencies and variations from these tendencies. Although he begins with the reservation that trade union theory does not lend itself to "rigorous" treatment, he nevertheless presents an analysis accompanied by conclusions concerning the trends which he postulates. He divides his analysis initially into general tendencies and the long-run trends which grow out of the processes of internal trade union development and external integration.

The processes of internal change develop long-run trends toward internal stability, centralization, and machine control; the processes of external integration encourage a long-run tendency toward accommodation, orderly and peaceful arrangements, and breadth and moderation. (p. 107)

The short-term deviations from these long-run trends are neither regular in their occurrence nor restricted to certain industries or geographic regions. Periods of trade union ferment occur, but generally level off to a stage of equilibrium. Public sentiment, union rivalry, strike trends, and technological change all cause these deviations but also give rise to stabilizing factors which restore the equilibrium of the long-run trends.

Lester enumerates seven long-run trends in the evolution of trade unions in America. These trends have occurred in labor history and will continue to occur in the future. They are as follows: (1) with union development comes psychological aging, and the greater the extent of a union's membership the greater the extent of the aging; (2) central control within a union engulfs democracy at the local level; (3) union leaders become administrators, and the result is a decrease in the differences between management's and the union's top officers; (4) unions lose their dynamism and their innovative tendencies as they succeed in their programs; (5) there is a decrease in the differences between white-collar and blue-collar unions, and the areas of worker protest are reduced; (6) differences between unions and other societal organizations decrease; and (7) conditions productive of militancy tend to decrease as union leaders assimilate into society, and the leaders act as moderating influences.

As regards short-term movements which generate change, Lester concluded that (1) they do not alter long-run changes although they do generate directions; (2) external developments may produce dynamic upswings; (3) short-run and long-run factors merge, thus producing stability; and (4) upswings tend to be less important as time passes (pp. 105–13).

Lester's theory of the long-run tendencies of trade union development is somewhat comparable to Robert Michels's concept of the "iron law of oligarchy." Although Michels's subject was political parties, his analysis is relevant to the study of trade unionism. He concluded that a group that had attained control of an instrument of "collective power" would do everything possible to maintain themselves in power. Oligarchy is "a preordained form of the common life of great social aggregates," and the leaders of a movement eventually become detached from the mass of the membership. "Those who stay on top push the others under."[2]

Lester qualified his conclusions as to the long-run and short-run portions of his theory. It was not his intent to develop a scheme that accurately predicted the short-term developments within a specific trade union; his analysis is both too general and too abstract for any type of applied, detailed application. In the case of the long-run tendencies, he recognized that both labor and management might object to them for the same reason. Personal experience may cause them to

> doubt that the dynamic qualities of unions tend to diminish; in their view the thrust of unionism to expand and make new conquests continues and seems likely to remain unabated. Many managements still fear invasion of their prerogatives, and many labor leaders point to the variety of anti-union activities still present in different sectors of the economy. At the same time, persons loyal to the union ideal may question whether fundamental changes have occurred within the American labor movement as a whole. (pp. 113–14)

In dealing with the collective bargaining function of trade unions, Lester forecasts three probable trends: (1) experience with collective bargaining will cause the process to become more professional in nature, largely because of the complexity of the issues which will arise; (2) with the increased emphasis on the collective bargaining process, a greater amount of time and effort will be devoted to contract administration and enforcement, especially with the trend toward longer term contracts; and (3) since bargaining has a tendency to compromise differences, the increased maturity accompanying this process will cause the use of the strike weapon to diminish.

In integrating the process of developmental change into theories of the labor movement, at least three approaches are possible. The first is to be content with a loose framework "which makes no pretence at prediction." A second alternative is to develop a separate theory of trade unionism for each stage along the union evolutionary scale. Finally, an attempt could be made to create an all-embracing theory of trade unionism and its evolution (pp. 119–23, 132–33).

Mark van de Vall[3]

Mark van de Vall analyzes the role and functioning of trade unions in a modern, postcapitalistic setting. He calls this new environment the welfare state. After an initial contention about the birth of the labor movement, he describes the economic, sociological, psychological, and political changes which coincide with the development of the welfare state. This is followed by an examination of the functions unions perform in advanced industrial society.

The environmental conditions which brought about the birth of the labor movement were industrialization, the capitalism of the 1800s, and the class conflict which accompanied these two developments. But these environmental variables have been drastically altered, and as a corollary, trade unions have also changed. Unions have undergone a process of integration into existing societies, and are no longer opposition movements but organizations which are entrenched in the economic and political functioning of society.

> In view of these alterations, we may ask whether the Western labor movement is still a child of its time, as it was in the last century. In other words, can we still explain the structure and functions of the labor movement in terms of a confrontation with its environment. (p. 1)

On the economic front, industrialization has led to prosperity. A redistribution of incomes has occurred, lessening social inequality. This leveling process is one of the most significant developments affecting trade unions in the twentieth century. The prosperity which has accompanied industrial and economic development has led to a consideration of the effect of trade unionism upon the income structure, and it has been concluded that collective bargaining has only a slight direct effect on income distribution. The ability of unions to raise the level of real wages has been called into doubt; but trade unions have been able to exert influence on the political front, which has had a dramatic leveling effect on the redistribution of incomes.

Trade unions have played an essential and creative role in governmental attempts at economic planning and in the establishment of the social programs which distinguish the welfare state. The political effectiveness of unions in establishing and running these programs is an accepted fact and "our conclusion is that, with regard to income equalization, economic unionism is less effective than political unionism" (p. 12). Additionally, changes in the ideology of both business and labor have resulted in a closer relationship between the two, and this has had an effect upon the relationship between the unions and the income structure. Economic leveling is seen by industry as increasing consumer buying power, and this coincides with labor's advocacy of it as a social good. This has all been made possible by labor's acceptance of the existence of "sociocapitalism," an attitude that marks the major difference between unions in the affluent welfare state as compared to those in the last century.

Sociologically, the number of individuals who are employees has increased dramatically, and manual workers are emulating the lifestyle of the middle class. This middle-class outlook dominates society; it has spread not only through blue collar acculturation but also through the growth of the white-collar population.

This heterogeneous white-collar population can be broken down into a lower level of employees whose economic status is not far above that of blue-collar workers, and an intermediate level of occupations ranging from bookkeepers to physicians. The lower and intermediate levels of the white-collar segment of the population comprise "the sociological core of the new middle class." Leveling effects are also evident in this class as a result of a multitude of social processes, and this process has taken place at the material, social, and psychological levels. Accompanying the decline of social and economic privileges, there is a more marked decrease in differences caused by increased education. In yet another leveling process, civil servants are finding that they no longer occupy a privileged position in comparison to private employees in regard to such things as "social security benefits and promotion prospects" (pp. 3, 7, 10–14, 16–17, 20, 22, 24–26).

It has also become more difficult to identify the higher level of the middle class. Consisting of only about 5 percent of the population of a welfare state, this group has continued to maintain a social distinction among themselves and has been less affected by the leveling process than have the lower and intermediate levels.

> Although material equalization . . . is hitting this group hardest, its effect is offset by expense accounts, status symbols, a large number of subordinates, and the social power conferred by their position. Unlike what has happened in the intermediate group, the individual character of their work has hardly been reduced at all. (p. 27)

To the exasperation of the trade-union movement, the modern white-collar worker does not display any sympathetic attitude toward blue-collar workers or their organizations. Although unions of professional employees do exist in Western

Europe, they differ noticeably from blue-collar unions. In spite of the fact that the total number of professional unions in a country is often large, they are small in numbers, and their primary concern is with their own limited interests—material betterment and the development of a multitude of rules specific to the profession—rather than with society as a whole. Finally, they are noted for the absence of any discernible political ideology.

A greater proclivity for joining unions resembling those of blue-collar workers exists among the lower level of the white-collar labor force, and a greater percentage of employees is organized at the lower level than at the intermediate and higher levels. The opportunity for personal mobility at the intermediate level is one of the major reasons for a lack of interest in organization. Among this group, a desire to pursue their self-interests collectively is not automatically converted into a desire to join a trade union. Added to this is the fact that employers are generally opposed to these workers who join or form unions, and the economic status of such an employee is intertwined with the company that provides employment (pp. 27–32).

Psychologically, a dramatic change has taken place in the mentality of the worker. There is less tendency to identify one's future with collective action, ideals, and organizations, and an increased concern with an individual's "own personal affairs"; there is also a growing awareness of the possibilities for individual advancement. The benefits provided by the welfare state have replaced the necessity for the provision of these needs by a trade union. Structural changes in industry, integrating the employee more closely to the firm, have added to the dramatic effect of psychological changes on trade unions. Individuals see themselves more closely tied to the enterprise with regard to income, dependency for employment (with a corresponding lack of mobility), and future prospects. This increased internal integration into the industrial community creates doubt as to the appropriateness of an external group like a union.

Politically, the historical ties between trade unionism and socialism have been weakened both ideologically and functionally. The development of the welfare state has meant that many of the social goals professed by socialism have been accomplished. This accomplishment cannot, however, be equated with socialism, as capitalist institutions and structures have been maintained. The welfare society has developed a plural power structure which has negated much of the strength of the previously held trade union "isms." Trade unions and employers' associations have become thoroughly integrated into the economic and political decision-making process along with the ruling government. The appearance of a new style of manager exhibiting trained expertise has increased the possibility of an infusion of industrial democracy where a single authority formerly ruled.

The accomplishments of the trade union movement have, in fact, resulted in a destruction of its former ideals. Because they are now able to achieve their aims through existing social orders, unions have lost many of the ideological foundations which formerly held them together. The survival of the ideologies of yesteryear may not be doomed, however. While the welfare state has accomplished many of the goals trade unions have advocated, van de Vall introduces the caveat that economic and political power remains concentrated in small groups of elites who still rule these social democracies (pp. 34–38, 41–46, 50).

Van de Vall begins his examination of trade union structure and function by citing the difficulty of defining unions; as an example of this complexity he offers Robert Hoxie's statement that the "union problem is a complex of economic, legal, ethical, and social problems which can be understood only by knowing the viewpoint of organized labor in all its riches, diversity, contradictions and shifting character." Van de Vall then quotes the following, written in 1959, as an example of a simplistic attempt to define unionism: "Trade unions are associations of workers who by means of collective bargaining endeavour to improve their working conditions, and economic and social position" (p. 53).

He claims that both definitions are too narrow in their scope; Hoxie's list of problems can, he thinks, be extended. While both definitions limit union activities and aspirations to organized workers, van de Vall maintains that unions, representing a minority of the labor force, achieve gains which benefit workers outside of union labor's ranks. He further disagrees with the notion that the sole concerns of a union are the interests of its membership.

But unions have widened their concerns sometimes even to the extent of supporting the needs of the national economy against the demands of their members. Modern trade unions are multi-purpose organizations whose goals for society increasingly take precedence over goals for the union membership. (p. 53)

In addition to acting merely on behalf of their membership, trade unions in advanced industrial societies increasingly tend to change their structure and function so as to act on behalf of all workers, industry, and society.

The ideals of the labor movement have traditionally broadened the outlook of its membership, and in the welfare state this has been translated into a diminution of the class war. The reduction of former class or political conflict to the enterprise or industrial level has given unions the opportunity to become involved in "issues of national scope." As a result, they have assumed new functions which have increasingly integrated them into the welfare state, and now function on the policy-making level in matters which benefit their members indirectly. This, of course, has created a dilemma for the integrated union: direct methods benefit their members in a most vivid way, but by becoming involved in broader issues and functions they benefit both their members and the population in general. The choice between the two methods is a difficult one, and unions run the risk of losing their identity in acting on behalf of society.

Modern unions are also aware of conditions facing the industry with which they bargain, and often act in concert with management on matters which are vital to "their" industry. This trend is illustrated by the restructuralization from craft to industrial unionism. Industrial unions are in a better position to mitigate the demands of their membership because of an awareness of problems facing industry. The creation of joint consultation in industry is an example of just such a trade union attitude and activity.

One attitude of trade unions toward joint consultation is that cooperation reinforces the common goals of labor and management. In addition, it gives workers and their representatives a legitimate right to a say in the determination of nonwage matters. Joint consultation has not, however, become firmly entrenched in Western European labor relations.

A second group of unionists holds that even in the welfare state "labor and management have no common goals." While unions that display a cooperative attitude deal with matters that extend beyond negotiations, those adhering to the "conflict theory" view joint consultation as a mere extension of collective bargaining and the union contract.

In a third approach, trade unions in the welfare state become involed in actions that benefit both members and nonmembers alike. By relating the level of their wage demands to the level of unemployment, unions apply pressure upon governments to maintain a policy of full employment. Thus the very nature of collective bargaining is changing from conflict to accommodation, taking account of variables internal and external to the bargaining process.

Because of the programs of the welfare state, union activities on behalf of the interests of their members are decreasing, "being transferred to other institutions," and their actions on behalf of both industry and society are expanding. But this adjustment to the environment of the welfare state undermines the value of trade union membership in the eyes of the workers, who had become accustomed to unions' directly protecting and pursuing the interests of their membership (pp. 54–64, 69, 73, 77, 85).

Industrialism and Industrial Man[4]

The authors of *Industrialism and Industrial Man* have constructed a model of industrial and economic development in which the independent variable is the elite that leads the drive for industrialization. In developing a "logic of industrialism" and a model of pluralistic industrialism, they also predict the future structure and functioning of labor organizations.

Recognizing the invincibility of industrialization does not mean approval of the process; nevertheless, the path toward industrialization is firmly established. While the process assumes many different forms, it produces a commonality wherever it occurs. This logic of industrialization portends many alterations for preindustrial societies. Among these imperatives are the development of an industrial work force (and this requires individual mobility); the establishment of educational systems; and a labor force differentiated by occupation, schedules of remuneration, and a multiplicity of both rights and duties in the enterprise—in short, a structured labor force. The scale of society expands in size, and urban areas predominate. Government plays a much larger role than it did in preindustrial society, and a web of rules is developed to regulate productive processes. Industrialization also creates a societal consensus that draws together individuals and groups, and an integrated value system is established.

As societies industrialize, the positions of order givers and order takers are created, and industrial workers form organizations to protect their interests. Systems of industrial relations are created as a necessary correlate to the complexities of industrial production. These systems establish authority relationships, and mechanisms are created to deal with the protests that inevitably rise from workers acting through their organizations. The authors of *Industrialism and Industrial Man* have purposely avoided "the term 'labor union' . . . to escape the implications that worker organizations generally are necessarily similar to the middle-class type of 'trade union' " (p. 193). They classify worker organizations according to the type of ruling elite under which the process of industrialization takes place—the middle class, dynastic leaders, colonial administrators, revolutionary intellectuals, or nationalist leaders—and examine them under seven categories: "(1) their ideology, (2) the functions of labor organizations, (3) the degree of labor organization participation in setting and administering the web of rules, (4) the extent of competition among labor organizations, (5) the structure of these organizations, (6) their sources of funds, and (7) the sources of leadership" (p. 194).

In the industrialization process, certain choices face both labor organizations and industrializing elites. In spite of their universality, these alternatives are most important to nationalist elites and to labor organizations at early stages of industrialization. The four questions which predominate are: "(1) wages vs. capital formation; (2) strikes vs. production; (3) grievance-handling vs. discipline; and (4) organization prestige vs. political subservience" (p. 201).

> Industrialization, whatever the source, characteristically redesigns and reshapes its human raw materials. The drastic changes in human beings and their relationships required to achieve a settled industrial work force have been made only with significant reactions from the workers-in-process. (p. 166)

The impact of the industrialization process upon its human actors has created many different responses. The authors term the negative responses to industrialization "worker protest," and they find that as the process evolves, the amount of protest declines.

Industrialization implies certain repercussions for the labor force of a country. The first of these is the destruction of pre-existing skills—a process that has been described by many writers—and the creation of new ones. The latter are demanded by the new industrial order at an ever-increasing rate, creating uncertainty and the formal organization of workers into trade unions. The web of rules thus created becomes more definitive and formalized, and the dominant trend is toward increased complexity. The disruptiveness of this tendency causes managers to seek out a justification for the governance of industry. The workers' unrest is intensified by the increasing concentration of the populace into urban areas. Urbanization breaks down the bonds which held preindustrial society together, and this often becomes the focus for revolt.

During the evolution of the industrialization process, a distinction develops between industrial and political conflict. This may be taken as a sign of maturity on the part of worker organizations, although economic and political forms of protest may exist simultaneously. The critical period of worker protest takes place early in the industrialization process, reaching a peak and then declining. With the evolution of the process, unorganized protest assumes an organized form, and worker organizations emerge. These organizations develop a viable power base in society and become both centralized and legitimate. In spite of this formalization of worker protest, however, the manifestations of industrial unrest continue to erupt in destructive forms, although collaboration between labor and management predominates (pp. 166–91).

The great transformation in society caused by industrialization has effects which go beyond the enterprise. Industry's authority structure creates new centers of power and increases the complexity of individual and group existence. Central to this pervasive alteration in consumption, production, culture, and living standards is the relationship between the managers and the managed—the order givers and the order takers. The role which an individual plays in his working life goes beyond the work place, for even the managers are managed, and the hierarchy of relationships is complex.

Industrialization creates a series of variables leading to conformity—to a new order which is that of pluralistic industrialism. Ideologies are eroded. Idealism is replaced by realism. Institutions arise to resolve differences between formerly warring factions and to prevent disruptions which hinder economic progress. The resulting "new realism" is basically conservative in nature. While change in the system is gradual and orderly, groups are still able to preserve and pursue their interests and positions. They develop veto power over any action which threatens their power position in society, or, even more basic, their survival. This power is exercised through institutionalized mechanisms of negotiation. Dialogue takes the place of dramatic action. Thus a balance between societal groups is maintained, and this is favorable to individual liberty and social mobility. Conflict between ideologies is institutionalized and consensus develops.

Another unifying force under pluralistic industrialism is the technology of such a society itself. As modern technology replaces outmoded forms of production, differences among nations are reduced. Technology is dynamic, calling for constant change. Highly structured labor markets arise to deal with rising skill levels. These and other forms of progress call for uniformity between societies. As progress in education is a necessary correlate of industrialization, a need arises for a literate, trained population. Education has several side effects, notably a new equality based on increased skills and reduced income differentials. Thus a new type of freedom, and a new demand for it, accompanies increased education.

The role of the state will also be altered. The government combines with management and labor organizations to establish the web of rules by which private and public enterprises are run, and thus acquires a vested role in labor-management relations; it also "becomes responsible for the general rate of growth, the level of economic activity, the distribution of power, the settlement of conflicts, and the prevention of economic or other sabotage of the economy by special interest groups" (pp. 221–30).

Pluralistic industrialism thus refers to societies in which no one group (or individual) is predominant, and it requires the centralization of the control function of society. One of the three power groups in society (along with government and management) is made up of worker organizations, which have the commonality of occupation or profession. The relationship between these organizations and their membership will be regulated by the government. The degree of organization will be as widespread as possible; individuals will have an incentive to form or join such labor organizations because of their role in creating the rules under which a person works.

Conflict will continue to exist between labor and management, but it will assume a more bureaucratic and less open form. As differences in ideology subside, the conflict that occurs will take the form of pressure tactics and persuasion. Once the consensus of a pluralistic society has been reached, labor organizations will lose their class identity, cease to be industrial in nature, and become centered around occupations. Their purpose will be narrowly defined and engrossed in self-interest. They will resist change in their occupation or profession and will act in a manner reminiscent of the conservative craft unions of the industrial era. Bureaucratic organization will be the means they will use to preserve their existing status. Individual identification will surround an occupation or profession rather than an industry or a class. "The occupational interest group will represent the employee in his occupational concerns and the occupation will draw his allegiance" (p. 236). Individuals will be free to choose their calling, but it will be the organization that governs the conduct of the job.

William A. Westley and Margaret W. Westley[5]

The basic assumption made by Westley and Westley in their study of the modern worker is that changes in the economic, social, psychological, and cultural environment of workers in both North America and the industrialized nations of Western Europe have had the effect of creating a new type of wage or salary earner. Different views have been developed of the worker both as an individual and on the job. A new concept of society has accompanied this. The Westleys concentrate their efforts on workers who have been most subject to the introduction of new technology and creative economic changes, and they further limit themselves to the young worker (under 35) who has been most affected and more closely represents the new, emerging worker (pp. 1–2).

In dealing with mass consumption society, they claim that income redistribution has made the group receiving "middle-range incomes" larger than those at the top or the bottom of the income scale. Higher income produces a feeling of security on the part of an individual and creates a preference for durable goods. The affluent society created by this income redistribution is characterized by increased leisure expenditures and a corresponding increase in leisure industries. Mass-consumption societies upgrade the role of the consumer in governmental and industrial drives for economic growth.

The ability to participate in this mass-consumption society allows workers to find an escape "from demeaning or frustrating work," and from the former social stratification which defined these individuals as less worthy because of the function they performed in society (pp. 7, 9, 16, 18).

Social and technical mobility has been enhanced by increased levels of, and opportunities for, education. The younger, more educated worker is more likely to have greater earning power when productive processes become automated. This increase in educational levels may be expected to have repercussions on the attitudes of these emerging workers toward unions, the role of government, and politics. Greater education results in a greater awareness of the impact of government, a greater awareness of politics, increased political information, a wider range of interests on political matters, greater participation in political discussions, a greater sense of freedom to discuss political issues with a wider range of individual types, and an increased sense of ability to influence government. The more highly educated worker is also more likely to be an active member of some sort of organization and to have greater confidence in his "social environment" (pp. 35–36).

The corresponding trust in his fellow human beings makes an educated worker more likely to act in a collective manner. It also increases an individual's self-confidence, so that he feels able to alter the union's policies and to change its leadership. It is not by chance that the greatest criticism of American union policies comes from younger members who do not have the anti-intellectual prejudice of their elders. It is true that an important part of trade union commitment has been an identification with the working class, and that education erodes the basis of this allegiance. On the other hand, increased levels of education have produced a brand of worker who is more able and more willing to participate in the democratic procedures of unions, industry, and country. This, of course, does not promise greater industrial or political tranquility; in fact, the emerging worker has shown himself to be more prone than the less educated worker to enforce his demands by aggressive action.

Affluence in societies is possible only with high levels of technology, and it creates a fluid rather than a stable worker. Labor-management relations are also influenced by technological change and automation, especially in the relationships among workers and between the managers and the managed. The basic attitude of the "traditional" worker toward the effects of technological change and automation is likely to be negative because of the uncertainty thus created. These changes do bring about certain equalizing factors by causing a decrease in the number of job classifications and pay differentials. They also cause work to lose its meaning for the worker. Self-fulfillment through work is no longer possible; work becomes simply a means to a higher standard of living.

The most significant effect of technological change will be felt among lower-level white-collar workers, whose work will become less distinguishable from factory work because of improvements in the factory environment. While automation involves an increase in status and pay for the manual worker, it means a corresponding decrease in these two factors for the clerical worker, who is typically female, while the factory worker is male (pp. 29, 35–39, 41–54).

The future also holds the realization of changes in labor mobility. Workers will move toward higher prestige jobs, which are expanding in numbers. "Just as the economy has raised the income levels for almost all workers, so it has raised the prestige level of most of the jobs available" (p. 62). The change in lifestyles which will result from these tendencies may not decrease the desire of the worker for recognition on the job. A conflict exists between this need for recognition and the tendency of work to become a means to an end. While technological change will make possible a richer off-the-job life, it may not make work itself more meaningful.

The emerging worker creates numerous problems for trade unions, the most immediate one being a disinclination to join. The changing structure of the labor force, "enlightened" managerial policies, and declining identification with the working class has resulted in a decrease in union power in modern society. Trade unions must constantly demonstrate to their membership their effectiveness in obtaining improvements on the job, and technological change increases the difficulty of this. In fact, increased labor costs resulting from union wage bargaining may give management further incentives to introduce automated or labor-saving mechanisms. Automation also decreases the effectiveness of strikes, the only weapon in a trade union's arsenal. This further adds to a union's difficulty in delivering the goods.

Weaknesses in a trade union's bargaining position vis-à-vis management and in its political influence are added to by changes in the composition of the membership itself. Younger workers who are more highly educated weaken the solidarity of labor. They comprise a new breed of workers "who hold self-conceptions, expectations, and attitudes that differ greatly from those of their leaders. Some may react to disappointment in their unions with alienation, others with rebellion" (p. 99). Where bargaining takes place on an industry or national scale, agreements which are reasonable at this level may not be so at the local level. This intensifies the rebellious nature of the emerging worker.

Other sources of union weakness, resulting from the coinciding developments of technological change and the emergence of a new type of younger and more educated worker, arise from the fact that trade unions are no longer able to count on the automatic loyalty of the rank and file in exerting their collective influence. Increased opportunities for upward mobility and affluence add to this development. Changing political attitudes are a result of higher levels of education, and they also place strains on the ties of the past. While the internal rifts initially weaken the position of the union, the increased emphasis on consumption may ultimately lead to a new source of trade union militancy based on the desire for the old nonideological trade union goal of "more." The Westleys exhibit mixed feelings toward the development of new forms of trade union militancy, but they accept the desire for material gains as "an important part of the structure of our economy. Unfortunately, we cannot have the advantages of this kind of urge without its disadvantages" (p. 101).

Unions are likely to develop problems in their dealings with white-collar workers. While the term "white collar" does not refer to a discrete group of workers, it does indicate a category of workers whose status is based upon tradition. While these workers are more susceptible to the programs of trade unions as technology alters their status within an enterprise, their numbers are decreasing. Still, the end result will be an increase in union membership at the lower level of the white-collar hierarchy.

White-collar workers are concerned with a broader range of issues than are blue-collar workers. Professional employees are concerned with maintaining their professions' standards, and there exists a feeling among all white-collar workers that work should "offer both interest and challenge." Beyond these two issues, the authors find little difference between the demands of white-collar and blue-collar workers. But differences in attitudes do exist, and are likely to cause internal difficulties for trade unions, for white-collar workers are more reluctant to strike, and they also wish to maintain the traditional distinction between themselves and the blue-collar labor force. Thus white-collar workers are likely to be supportive of the economic, collective actions of trade unions, but only so long as these organizations are able to demonstrate an ability to obtain benefits and gains which the white-collar workers are unable to achieve on their own.

Problems are likely to develop in industrial relations because of the emerging worker. Two basic causes of conflict are built into the system of labor-management relations: the established authority system and the control over the distribution of financial rewards. Since these two phenomena exist in all employment relationships, conflict must be viewed as inherent in industrial relations, and the expression of this conflict should be regarded as a sign of health. The Westleys' concern is not with industrial conflict itself, but with the issues which underlie this conflict.

The two basic issues that erupt into conflict in an automated society arise between management's right to organize work in the most efficient manner possible and the right of workers to control their work situations; that is, the conflict between productivity and job security. Rapid technological change has made this problem more acute, and it represents a threat to the worker who is trying to transform his job into a career. Mechanisms for the defense of job security and employment have been developed by workers acting through their organizations which restrict the ability of management to make use of changes in the technology of production. Here the new feeling of equality which the emerging worker holds as part of his essence arises as an issue.

The second major cause of conflict is the contrary demands of increased productivity (and the resulting higher wages) and the worker's desire for job security and fear of unemployment. This issue becomes especially acute when skills are made obsolete. In spite of these challenges facing collective bargaining, it is likely to remain the primary device for settling disputes between labor and management. While increased centralization and joint consultation may improve the effectiveness of collective bargaining, it does not alter the fact that there is no over-whelming drive to take into account the concerns of the public. But the interests of society will best be served by leaving labor and management relatively free to settle their own disputes.

In addition to the economic nature of the emerging worker and his inclination toward trade union membership and ac-tion, the Westleys deal with his political outlook. They con-clude that, especially in the United States and Canada, the emerging worker with his new middle-class orientation will tend to be more conservative in his voting patterns and less likely to affiliate with political parties or political movements "with a strong working-class bias." The worker is currently less conscious of his affiliation with any sort of working class, and he views the future with optimism. His lifestyle and work experience exhibit an increasing egalitarianism, and internal trade union apathy or rebellion indicate that these organiza-tions "have failed to keep up with this change" (pp. 97–113).

The Westleys find stress resulting from the experience of the modern, emerging worker. He has little respect for what he considers to be the outdated older leadership of his union, especially since he never fought in early battles for recogni-tion which were important in developing trade union loyalty. Instead, the bureaucratic measures which he has acquired as a result of his extended education lead him to place an in-creased value on "the rationally competent and technologi-cally knowledgeable." He rejects the goals and policies which the older leader has set up and presents at the bargaining table. This dissatisfaction often leads to wildcat strikes or al-terations in the methods of participation in union affairs. "Whereas the older leader was a mass politician, using and abusing the mass meeting to achieve his ends, the modern worker will prefer bureaucratic politics, the meetings of ex-perts, and the effective committee" (p. 118).

John H. Goldthorpe et al. [6]

A trilogy of studies performed in the late 1960s in Great Brit-ain relate solely to the situation in that nation rather than attempting to build a general model. These studies sought to examine preconceived notions about the affluent worker in the context of his industrial employment; that is, the *embour-geoisement* of the working class into middle-class society. The main objective of the researchers was to test empirically "the thesis that, as manual workers and their families achieve relatively high incomes and living standards, they assume a way of life which is more characteristically 'middle class' and become in fact progressively assimilated into middle-class society" (*IAB*, p. 1). In the course of this project they developed an empirically tested schematic design of the role of workers and their trade unions, and the social, economic, and political roles which these unions play in an "allegedly" transformed environment.

Among the multitude of relationships they sought to examine, this team of researchers concerned themselves with the attitudes and behavior toward their unions displayed by the "affluent" workers surveyed. They sought to differentiate between the newly affluent workers and the more "traditional" type of manual employee—not necessarily as to their degree of "participation in union affairs," but in the form of this participation and its meaning for the individual worker. Beginning with the assumption that trade unionism has represented a device for economic improvement as well as a broader movement seeking drastic alterations in industry, they correctly held that British trade unionism has meant more to its members than economic betterment. It has traditionally been seen as a form of collective action based on solidarity, seeking the sociopolitical reformation of society as a whole. The extent to which these wider ideals have decreased in importance was given the greatest significance in the study.

The most important questions concerning British unionism have traditionally surrounded the issues of authority and power, both within industry and in society generally. Trade unions have thus sought to increase the role of the workers within their place of employment and in the political arena through the Labour Party. The survey examined attitudes of workers toward both of these activities, and found that the majority of the workers felt that trade unions should limit themselves to the role of combatants on the economic front. Only craft workers retained the notion that workers should play a larger role in the actual running of the enterprise. The majority opinion expresses the workers' notion of work as a means to an end and their unwillingness to share responsibility for the management of their firm. This is an illustration of what has been termed "limited-function" trade unionism.

Related to this idea of limited function unionism is the finding that these affluent workers did not see themselves as part of a broader, all-encompassing labor movement. They rejected the coordinated functioning of the trade union movement and the Labour Party as the integrated wings of a socially conscious and reformistic labor movement. Further evidence of workers' failure to identify with their unions outside of the job site is their feeling that the organizations to which they belonged were too powerful on a national level.

This orientation of the affluent workers toward their unions is reflective of their attitude toward their work in general. With the exception of craft workers, who seek more from their work and their unions than economic betterment, the majority of the affluent workers have created a new type of unionism which, consistent with their expectations of their work, provides solely economic benefits. However, the authors are quick to point out that even economically oriented unionism represents for workers, industry, and society "an important form of collective action" (IAB, pp. 113–15). This proclivity still remains an essential attitude of manual workers who sell their labor, however affluent they may be.

The intensity of working-class consciousness was also a subject of the empirical research making up the second part of the trilogy. Both white- and blue-collar workers agreed that big businessmen held too much societal power, and that separate laws for the rich and the poor existed in British society. By a small majority, the blue-collar workers agreed with the white-collar workers surveyed that the Labour Party and the trade unions should be kept apart as separate entities. Generally, there was little difference in the working-class orientation of the affluent blue-collar workers and the white-collar workers. While union membership is important to the affluent blue-collar worker, his "style" of trade unionism is one of instrumental collectivity. The trade union is used as a means to improve an individual's standard of living; it is not viewed as an instrumentality for "transforming the social structure," or for providing a greater role for workers in the management of the firm. While the affluent worker identifies with the Labour Party as the political organization most closely representing his vested interests, trade unions exist for the narrow purpose of making economic gains on the job site.

The empirical evidence indicates that attitudes toward the Labour Party are formed from an individual's position as a manual worker, and that affluence leading to a middle-class lifestyle does not lead to a decline in the propensity to vote Labour. Loyalty to the Labour Party is just one expression of what the authors have termed "solidaristic collectivism" (*PAB*, pp. 25–28, 73–75). Affluence, it seems, does not breed individualism.

In their last study, the researchers point out that the thesis of the increasing *embourgeoisement* of the working class gained considerable popularity after the victories of the Conservative Party in the 1950s. However, they were unable to discover any evidence that manual workers, both the traditional and the newly affluent, were rejecting the norms of the working class and accepting those of the white-collar workers or the middle class.

Focusing on three major aspects of the lives of the affluent workers which have a "crucial bearing on the thesis of *embourgeoisement*," they discovered that middle-class lifestyles were not consciously followed. These variables—work, patterns of sociability, and aspirations and social perspectives— further revealed that assimilation into the society of the middle class is not occurring and is not desired. In spite of increased earnings and better working conditions, a worker remains an individual who sells his labor for a livelihood. The requirement of overtime work in order to obtain a degree of affluence further adds to this tendency. Class differences are not disappearing. While the lifestyles of workers able to enjoy increased consumption and reside in new communities do differ from workers restricted by economics to working-class communities, these affluent workers have not adopted middle-class norms or lifestyles. "Class and status relationships" do not entirely coincide with economic and technological changes (*CS*, pp. 22, 25, 157–63).

Although some writers claim that affluence is accompanied by an increasing identification with management on the part of the worker and by a decreased proclivity for collective means of obtaining economic goals, the results of the third study do not confirm this idea.

The growth of large-scale enterprises, in an area outside the older industrial regions of the country, was associated with a marked *strengthening* in union organisation. It would appear that workers attracted to these plants by the prospects of affluence still in a majority of cases joined unions even when this was not compulsory and when they had no previous commitment to unionism. (*CS*, p. 167)

The conclusion to be drawn from this is that the affluent worker finds union membership advantageous to his employment position. The fact that trade unions were used by these workers to pursue their own interests does not mean that the effectiveness of collective action on the part of manual workers is losing either its strength or its appeal.

The major political fact which emerges from this study is that politics still retains a link with class, and affluence does not reduce working-class attachment to Labour.

Fred C. Munson[7]

Although he was writing about Indian trade unions and not specifically attempting to develop a theory of unionism, Fred C. Munson developed a structure of trade union types which is relevant to the study of union behavior and function in modern society. In constructing his analysis, Munson differentiates among three kinds of trade unions: member-centered, dependent, and political. His basic premise is that those questioning a union's effect on society "ignore the fact that unions exist to serve their own interest, not someone else's." Unlike business institutions, unions have failed to develop advocates who claim that they are doing what is best for society as a whole when they are in fact performing this essential function.

One of the basic differences between a trade union and a business organization is that the flow of authority is "delegated upward," and thus the allegiance of the member to the union assumes critical importance. In order to develop this membership allegiance, a union must be able to demonstrate successfully that affiliation results not only in economic gains but also in noneconomic benefits that fill the worker's needs for dignity and decision-making power on the job site. Thus while a member's allegiance to a union is based on self-interest, this self-interest is made up of economic and noneconomic components (pp. 3, 7, 9).

The device which is essential for serving these self-interests is collective bargaining power. Munson uses the term member-centered unions for those which are able to function in this manner. A union without such power may still be able to exist, but becomes dependent upon support from some source external to the union itself (either the company with which it deals or the state). A price is extracted for this outside support, and the greater the degree of support, the greater is the dependence of the union on its source of aid. "Such unions lack the organizational bond which gives the basis for bargaining power which in turn encourages member-centered unions; unions without this basis for power will be called dependent unions" (p. 7).

There is a third type of trade union which is unable to fulfill its members' aspirations because of a lack of bargaining power. They are dependent, not on the company or the state, but on a political party. In the case of political unionism, as in the case of dependent unionism, the strong connection between the union leader and the outside organization may often mean that the union is in actuality a part of that outside organization. Political unionism seeks to serve a larger portion of society than its membership, and its leadership is committed to this function.

Such an ideology has the advantage of attracting fellow ideologues to the support of the organization, but leadership skills are in short supply. This support does have the advantage of drawing upon "free resources." But the major difference, or drawback, of such an arrangement is that service to the union's membership becomes secondary in nature and no longer an ultimate end. This, in fact, is the major distinguishing feature between member-centered and political unionism: the latter views the organization as a weapon in the class struggle.

Munson expresses a decided preference for member-centered trade unionism. Falling back on his initial definition, he dismisses the effectiveness of unionism existing as "an arm of the government" and as a subordinate part of the fight for political revolution. "Member-centered unionism is not literally best in a social sense. It is best in a definitional sense, for we mean by 'union' a grouping of persons with similar interests acting to achieve common goals" (p. 11). This definitional factor best characterizes the need for survival as an organization while recognizing the fact that the development of a stable form of trade unionism is dependent upon the existence of a stable industrial work force.

"Member-centered unionism does not have a single, uniform goal." While it is often identified with the achievement of more money for its membership, this is only one of many ways in which such a form of unionism may make a member's life more pleasant both on and off the job. Once employers have accepted the fact that they will have to deal with unions, an understanding of the employer's interests is necessary if a member-centered union is to obtain as many concessions as possible for its membership at the bargaining table. This type of employer-union relationship stresses the institutionalization of conflict. Management and union goals will become integrated, and the ultimate result is the assimilation of the institution of trade unionism into the existing society.

Andre Gorz [8]

Andre Gorz attempts to update Marxist doctrine in light of the failure of several accepted predictions of Marxism to develop. He notes the fact that the weakness of socialism in all capitalist nations has resulted in the failure to intertwine this program of change in the basic foundations of society to the concrete, immediate demands of the working class. Capitalism has not collapsed, and the polarization of society into two opposing classes has not occurred. In spite of this, he claims that the subordination of the gains which workers have made to the functioning of capitalist systems is not inevitable.

Subordinate powers absorb the workers into a responsibility-sharing role in the running of capitalist enterprise. Conversely, autonomous power means the ability of the workers to challenge the basic premises upon which capitalist management is based. Such autonomous power is an indispensable element in the necessary education of the workers which will allow them to visualize socialism as a practical and attainable goal. A strategy of the progressive assumption of power by the workers does not mean that a revolution is neither necessary nor inevitable. Since the increased impoverishment of the working class has not occurred, their conquest of power has not become "an immediate end in itself," but it must be made clear that it is a realizable end under systems of capitalism. Intermediate reforms must first be obtained, however, to illustrate to the working class that the ultimate goal of socialism is within reach.

All attempts to subordinate the union to the party must be fought. No limitation should be placed on trade union autonomy. The first reason for this assumption is economic in nature. Freedom from the pressure of trade unionism would allow enterprises the power to regulate industrial productivity and the workers' standard of living without restriction. Furthermore, the programs of trade unions directly reflect the needs coming from the productive processes and, in a broader context, from the social life of the working class. Organized trade union political action is the major method by which capitalism can be brought to a crisis. It gives substance to the tension between capital and labor and brings about the inability of capitalism "to implement the necessary structural reforms."

> Only in the union can socialist man be forged in the present: the worker organized with other workers to regulate production and exchange, the producer dominating the production process instead of being subordinated to it. (p. 18)

Mere economic confrontations between labor and capital no longer represent the "fundamental antagonism" which exists between these two classes. While the prediction of absolute impoverishment has not been fulfilled in regard to the economic standards of the working class, it does have meaning when interpreted in terms of the "social reproduction of labor power"—the change from poverty to misery. Demands for increased wages are no longer able to unify the mass of workers. This must be done through programs aimed at the disparity of power.

If solely economic battles weaken class consciousness, the horizons of the working class must be expanded to the political level. The struggle for the socialist transformation of society must be based on the fact that capitalist production has made the condition of the workers more intolerable in terms of alienation, exploitation, oppression, and dehumanization. It is the design of the capitalist to narrow the horizons of the workers to job-related matters in order to prevent an expansion of working-class consciousness.

In spite of the fact that most industries require a higher degree of technical training than was needed in the past, this has not resulted in greater worker control over the process of production. The use of economic rewards to compensate for this oppression is the direction which management would like to see unions take, for it allows the "mutilation" of the worker to continue unabated. While workers will encourage their unions to fight for concrete gains, they will not endorse drives for more power to give the union greater control over the work situation. "This is why the first task of the working class movement today is to elaborate a new strategy and new goals, which will indivisibly unite wage demands, the demand for control, and the demand for self-determination by the workers of the conditions of work."

A requirement for the creation of this new, aggressive strategy is the development of the autonomy of labor organizations which gives the workers the power to successfully challenge management. Such a strategy rejects union cooperation in the making of policy decisions (which would be class collaboration); instead, it provides the opportunity for workers to emancipate themselves from management control. A union must seek to negotiate over all parts of the work situation, creating an antagonistic power which is both a permanent and continuous challenge to management. Each partial victory of the unions increases both their power and their class consciousness. Workers will have taken the offensive. Trade unions will no longer merely be defensive organizations. The ultimate challenge which will result from such action is directed at the priorities and purposes of capitalist production (pp. 21–51).

This new program and strategy is necessary if the condition of the laborer at the work place is ever to be altered; if the meaning of an individual's working life is to change from one of capitalist-implemented alienation. The model of "affluent consumption" which has been offered is a disguise for the deprivation which monopoly capitalism imposes upon society. "On this subject, one can never emphasize sufficiently the fact that social, cultural, and regional underdevelopment on the one hand and rapid development of 'affluent' consumer goods industries on the other are two sides of the same reality" (p. 62). The private accumulation of wealth deprives the public of the surplus value which could be used for social investment. The primary aim of capitalist production is not social development; it is the production of goods with sole regard to maximum profit, disregarding utility. Work has ceased to be a creative activity and has become merely a means for the satisfaction of passive, material needs. Affluent consumption does nothing to challenge the basis for a worker's spiritual poverty, which is the alienation of labor.

In established capitalist economies, these unsatisfied human needs coexist with the waste resulting from the manner of production. The only situation in which competition creates technical progress is where such action also provides for maximum profits. Technical progress is centered around the needs of production, not the needs of the populace. This pursuit of maximum profit has no relationship to a pursuit of maximum use value. Profit is the sole criterion by which the importance of activities is measured.

The form of power which controls the modern capitalist society is technocratic power. The technocrats are not the representatives of monopoly capitalism, but they act as mediators between the interests of capitalism and the contradictory interests of society. They attempt to deny the need for the class struggle by the depoliticization of the proletariat. If a labor movement lacks an anticapitalist ideology, the technocrat will attempt to integrate unions into the existing mechanisms of the capitalist state. An anticapitalist labor movement aims at destroying the ideology which makes the technocrats functional. This allows them the chance to join with the labor movement, and have it serve as an "outlet for their competence" (pp. 55–83, 121–25).

Trade union cooperation has been an essential part of economic planning in the capitalist countries of Western Europe. These are attempts to further integrate the labor movement into the established institutions of capitalism, but labor's role in these planning schemes is always a subordinate one. They are attempts to "trap" the trade union movement into a position of willingly accepting resolutions to problems which conform to the logic of capitalism. At an international level, cooperative attempts at planning are even more destructive of the development of an anticapitalist ideology on the part of the labor movement. The trade union representatives on these planning councils are cut off from the workers they represent, and run the risk of becoming technocrats themselves. "European planning as presently conceived [the Common Market] is a new attempt to deprive the labor movement on the international level of the weapons which it still wields on the national level, and to enmesh it in capitalist logic" (p. 153).

In response to this challenge, the trade union movement must develop an international strategy to match capitalist internationalization. Only a united front which combines the strength of the unions of all countries involved can exercise true countervailing power at the international level. The resulting trade union pressure can be used to protect jobs by applying worker control through a coordinated effort at the international level. Such a united effort would also internationalize labor's defense of trade union autonomy and allow an international reorientation of priorities dealing with production and consumption.

Dual Labor Market Theory[9]

In dealing with the current and future role of the trade union movement, one group of theoreticians has focused on the multitude of formalized barriers that an individual faces in a highly structured labor market and has thus developed an interpretation of the labor market called dual labor market theory. The dual labor market is made up of a primary market, which performs the functions of training, recruitment, and promotion for the majority of the labor force, and a secondary market, which performs these functions for minority group members in American society (p. 67).

The terms "internal" and "external" labor market have also been used to deal with discrimination according to sex and age. The internal labor market consists of an enterprise in which the governance of the work force is determined by a series of rules, both substantive and procedural. These rules provide rights and privileges to employees in the firm or occupation and have an overriding concern with job protection. "The external labor market contains all other workers." Conditions outside of this structure may cause an enterprise or skill to take new workers into its ranks, but once this happens, the internal labor market rules govern. It is in this process of internal governance that trade unions fulfill their function.

A further distinction has been developed along the same lines alleging the existence of a primary sector and a secondary sector. The primary sector—which offers an individual better wages, working conditions, protection from management, and job stability than the secondary sector—is divided into an upper and a lower tier. The upper tier is made up of professionals, technocrats, and administrators. These positions, which are based on a body of theoretical knowledge, offer employees more in the way of pay, status, and promotional opportunities and call for more creativity and initiative than those in the lower tier. In the latter—skilled trades, clerical jobs, and sales positions—training is more specific in nature and is lacking in a theoretical basis.

The secondary labor force is made up of unskilled workers, nonfarm laborers, and service employees. These individuals tend to be teenagers with little work experience, adults with a history of low-paid jobs or poor work records, individuals "with clearly defined obstacles to employment—the aged, mothers with young children, students seeking part-time work, addicts, alcoholics, illiterates, and physically and mentally handicapped persons" (p. 68), and people who have sources of income such as welfare, which keep them out of the labor force.

Certain societal and economic factors help to maintain the duality of the labor market. The laborers' own uncertainty concerning the division of labor affects the skill distribution of jobs. The primary and the secondary sectors become both interdependent and antagonistic as work becomes more generalized in the upper tier and more routine in the lower tier of the primary sector and in the secondary sector. The result is that the poorly paid are restricted to positions in the secondary sector, where they become trapped because of the institutionalization surrounding occupations in the primary labor market (especially in the upper tier).

Employers have a vested interest in maintaining the stability in employment which results from this institutionalization. Trade unions also have a vested interest in the establishment of rules governing employment positions, and are supported by management in their efforts to obtain this stability. The entire legal foundation of labor-management relations in the United States, which seeks the institutionalization of conflict in employment situations through the mechanisms of the National Labor Relations Act, solidifies the "barriers between the two markets." According to dual labor market theory, basic social institutions cause the problem of unemployment because they freeze people into social positions.

Making use of dual labor market analysis, one discovers that an increasing number of jobs in the secondary labor market are service jobs. This has immense significance for developments in postindustrial society, for service-oriented economies consist primarily of secondary jobs.

The secondary labor market holds the promise of a new labor movement because workers structured into such positions are more fully aware of their alienation than is the case in the primary labor market. "It seems to be left to the minority groups in the United States to create the impetus for a significant workers' movement" (p. 380). While the trade unions as the organizers of the working class have the responsibility for taking the lead of establishing a better "work world," they have yet to do so. The typical union position is to react, not to plan and create.

This accounts for the low degree of union organization among the workers in the secondary labor market, who fail to see any benefits to be gained from such organization. However, as professional employees find their autonomy being threatened by increased bureaucracy, they are turning to the only source of power at their disposal—"the collective power of unionism." Through a union's ability to establish lines of authority, these professionals are able to clarify their autonomy. The influential role which unionized professionals are supposedly going to play as part of the service economy will be of minimal impact unless craft unions are restructured along industrial lines. An industrial union composed of all professional, skilled, unskilled, and clerical workers employed in an enterprise would have the power and ability to change working situations significantly. The collective power of union organization would thus be altered from the intense but concentrated occupational solidarity which characterizes professional unions "to the total administrative control of corporate groups."

Whether this will happen depends upon the leadership of trade unions. While labor leaders act as innovative bargainers in their dealings with management, they behave in an authoritative manner toward their members to protect their vulnerable leadership positions. The acceptance of trade unions and their leaders by society and by management has led to the increased conservatism of the labor movement and the end of labor's "radical potential." Centralization of function and power has accompanied this conservatism, and the modern trade union has become a bureaucratic hierarchy. Established union leadership has acted as a brake on real societal change, thus adding to the stagnation analyzed by the dual labor market theorists. It is their hope that the rise of a "significant workers' movement" will call for a new type of leadership (which, they admit, already exists in some established trade unions) (pp. 253–54, 176).

Daniel Bell[10]

The drastic alterations in the very basis of production and power in postindustrial society cause Daniel Bell to question whether trade unions will continue to play any real decision-making role in the new era into which the United States is evolving. He describes preindustrial societies as being engaged mainly in extractive industries, and he claims that this is the situation in which most of the world finds itself at present. In contrast, industrial societies are centered around the production of goods, and life becomes "a game against fabricated nature." The major distinction between an industrial society and a postindustrial society is that the latter is based upon the performance of services. The "game" that is played is therefore transformed into one between individuals.[11]

Information, and the access to information, become the keys to societal power, and the central focus is on the professional whose training allows him to provide the needs of a postindustrial society. Such a service-oriented economy involves several stages of evolution. An initial expansion in transportation and the use of energy is accompanied by an expansion in the nonmanufacturing blue-collar labor force. This is followed by the mass consumption of goods and an increase in services using white-collar workers. Finally, the tertiary sector, composed of personal services, expands, not in numbers only; the increased need for technocrats and professionals leads to the emergence of a "new intelligentsia."

Correlated to these developments is the fact that the largest sector of the economy in terms of the growth of employment has been the government at local, state, and federal levels. While this employment expansion engenders visions of a white-collar economy, it must be remembered that not all segments of a service economy are white collar in nature. Such expansion does, however, support the assertion that if manufacturing plays the major role in shaping the work force of an industrial, goods-producing economy, "then the United States is no longer an industrial society. The changeover to a postindustrial society is signified not only by the change in sector distribution—the places *where* people work—but in the pattern of occupations, the *kind* of work they do" (pp. 124–28, 133–34).

Western industrial society had three distinctive features: the emergence of the corporation as the dominant type of business enterprise, mechanization and its implications, and a "polarized" type of class conflict. None of these exists in a postindustrial society. Large organizations no longer predominate, as the majority of the firms which deal in services are relatively small. Even in the larger enterprises, small units within these organizations exercise a great degree of "professional control."

The implications of these transformations for trade unions are dramatic. Historically, the labor movement has been most successful in organizing blue-collar workers, who have served as the major source of labor's strength. With a shift toward white-collar employment, the power base of labor is threatened. The old social division of labor and capital is replaced by a new class structure based upon the axes of property and knowledge.

While the trade-union movement today is stronger than it has ever been when considered in terms of total numbers, it has been shrinking as a percentage of the total labor force. Having reached the saturation point in its two major areas of organizational extent—manufacturing and construction— the labor movement has demonstrated an unwillingness to tackle the number of smaller employers who remain unorganized. One reason is the costliness of this process; another is the traditional resistance of employees in white-collar jobs. The growth of both trade unionism and collective bargaining has always been dependent on the favorable support of government, and the role of the National Labor Relations Board was instrumental in institutionalizing industrial conflict through collective bargaining. More recently, however, the only "real" expansion in the organization of the unorganized has taken place among government workers. At the federal level, this has been the result of friendly executive orders and the result of comparable governmental action at the state and local levels (pp. 160–62, 41–42, 137–40). The major areas of white-collar employment remain unorganized, as do the professions.

Even though it comprises a smaller proportion of the total labor force, the blue-collar sector is becoming more homogeneous and better educated. The conditions of employment bear little resemblance to those which existed during the great upsurge of industrial unionism. But in spite of both economic and noneconomic improvements, the control of the work process itself lies beyond the control of the worker and his union. Furthermore, the unions have never really challenged the right of management to exercise this control and authority over workers. This raises yet-to-be-answered questions about the workers' reaction to this situation, especially the demands of a younger and more highly educated blue-collar labor force. If a new psychology is developing among these workers, the trade unions have yet to deal with it.

One truism about modern society is that few groups of employees remained unorganized for long. Professionals, both employed and self-employed, have been and still are organizing. Some occupational organizations have affiliated with the AFL-CIO. But the major question which will have to be answered as postindustrial society emerges is whether these organizations will remain traditional professional associations or become "militant and aggressive labor unions." It may be the younger professionals who turn these associations toward militancy to resist constraints placed upon the profession. While the organization of professionals will be a major characteristic of postindustrial society, the form which these organizations will assume, the programs they will pursue, and the manner in which they will pursue them still remain subjects for speculation.

In addition to the threat to organized labor resulting from the changes in the makeup of the labor force, competition from abroad may force American industry into a position of reduced ability to meet any new demands by younger workers for control of the work situation. Since these demands, as well as economic issues, raise the cost of labor, the result may be a squeeze upon employers which will cause them increasingly to resist the demands of trade unions.

Replacing the business executive as the dominant figure in American society will be the new intelligentsia. The values of the business community have had a pervasive effect upon American society, an effect which far exceeds the numbers of businessmen. In industrial society, the business community has received the greatest rewards, although it has had to share these economic rewards with organized labor. At the same time, its societal power has been restricted by trade unions through collective action and by government regulation. In postindustrial society, the decisions of the business executive, and correspondingly the unions dealing with him and his enterprise, will be subordinated to other power centers in society. Critical decisions will increasingly emanate from the government, and the use of advanced technological procedures will make the effects of these decisions more difficult to alter (pp. 144–45, 159, 344).

The pace and the scale of change which distinguish postindustrial from industrial society have both direct and indirect effects on the labor problems of the future. Bell admits that if one were to undertake a full-scale analysis of these labor problems it would "have to include the structure of trade unionism, the problem of bureaucracy and democracy in unions, and the like" (pp. 143, 160–64). He chooses not to deal with these matters, and instead restricts himself to changes in the composition of the labor force. He cites as its single most striking feature the higher level of education which its members will have attained. The greatest pressure for social change will, he believes, come from the highly educated worker employed in the nonprofit sector of the economy.

The dominance of the "labor issue," the conflict between employer and employee, has assumed precedence over conflicts arising from other social divisions in industrial society. But this conflict of interest between labor and management has become institutionalized, and it has not assumed the cataclysmic proportions which the radical theorists of the nineteenth and twentieth centuries predicted. This trend will continue in the future, and the "labor issue" is no longer central in a postindustrial society. Other issues, probably communal rather than parochial, will take its place as focal conflicts.

4

A Model of Trade Unionism
in Emerging Postindustrialism

The Role of Conflict

As we have seen, common interests in their work situation have caused industrial workers to develop formal organizations for the purpose of alleviating the conditions under which they toil. The organized strength of workers acting as a collectivity has forced employers to deal with their employees on job-related matters. Workers have used these collective means to enhance their on-the-job status and thus also affect their off-the-job status. This method which they have used is, of course, collective bargaining, which, as the Webbs pointed out, has replaced the use of the individual contract between employer and employee.

Having developed an economic power base at the employment level and established a common rule or web of rules, workers have used this economic power base as a means to exert influence on the polity. While the method of legal enactment has been used to a far lesser extent in the United States than in Western Europe, it has been made possible by the creation of an economic power base which neither legislatures, the courts, or other parochial interest groups (such as employers) can erode. Although they would have looked at such a development with different eyes, both Lenin and Perlman have proved to be correct. Left to themselves, workers will develop only trade unions of the type Lenin called *bourgeois;* that is, organizations with an economic power base seeking improvements in wages, hours, and other conditions of employment by dealing collectively with their employers.

Faced with the development of workers' economic organizations, governments were forced to establish the legislative means for allowing such collective organization to run its course. Not to do so meant the possibility of workers using their collective strength upon employers and society in a manner which would likely be disruptive rather than constructive and counterproductive to the reason for such organization—the establishment of a countervailing force to face the unilateral authority of employers. Established modes of government were thus able to prevent the "hardening of the class fronts."[1] The conflict which emerged from employment relationships led to structural changes in the economy, in the polity, and in society.

Contrary to the predictions of Norman Ware, economic unions have achieved far more than a mere wage policy; they have developed an extensive program for job control and security, and have, to a limited extent, sought the redistribution of income through political means in the United States. It is true that collective bargaining has been relied on as a much more effective means of redistributing income by obtaining wage gains for union membership—gains which have also served indirectly to increase the wages of the unorganized. Nevertheless, labor has not been as reluctant to use political methods as Perlman would have had us believe. Although he described accurately the AFL of 1928, when *A Theory of the Labor Movement* was published, he failed to predict the cooperation of trade union economic and political programs which have existed since the emergence of industrial unionism and the New Deal.

The results produced by industrial conflict must lead us to conclude "that every act of organization is as such a process of institutionalization."[2] The first effect which the organization of trade unions had upon society was to decrease in intensity and degree the amount of industrial conflict as collective bargaining on the part of workers became possible, for no employer could deal with an unstructured, unorganized, and unrelated group of employees. The democratic processes of society have been reinforced by the success of the negotiations between labor and management on job-related issues. As mentioned earlier, this has served the purpose of adding another organized vested interest group within the structural boundaries of a pluralistic democracy. The change did require some alteration in social structure, but still was able to take place within the scope of democratic processes.

One final result of the organization of trade unions and the establishment of collective bargaining has been the separation of industrial from political conflict. The leaders of industry are now able to influence a smaller portion of a worker's life than was the case in the distant past. While employers, acting independently or through their associations, are capable of exerting a great amount of political power, and in fact do so, they have lost the domination which they formerly held over the off-the-job rights and living style of their employees. As the effect of industry upon its employees has become less all-embracing, a separation has occurred between the worker as a political citizen and the worker as an economic citizen. With the infusion of a greater degree of pluralism into American society, an individual's membership in an industrial class can no longer be equated with his membership in a political class. This is strikingly demonstrated in Great Britain, where it is estimated that one out of every three trade union members votes Conservative. This political flexibility is increased as the authority structures of industry and government have become separated, and we now have government acting as the regulator of industry rather than as its spokesman.

Industrial conflict has thus become more purely industrial, and not political, conflict. As the issue of industrial conflict becomes more narrowly centered around the job and less concerned with the needs of society as a whole, the individual worker becomes more concerned with these issues in his role as worker (or employee) than he is in his role as political citizen or even as a consumer.[3] This separation between industrial and political conflict has pleased some and disturbed others, but it has occurred. The extent of this development can be seen when viewed side by side with the institutionalization of conflict. Each development has served to reinforce the other.

Thus industrial conflict has not played the role in the employment relationship that was predicted by the scientific socialists. If one accepts the theories of Marx and Lenin, it follows that the greater the extent of industrialization in a nation, the greater would be the degree of industrial conflict and the polarization of society into two armed camps, one growing in size as the other decreases. But, rather than leading to disruption, industrial conflict has united wage earners to deal with their employers in an economic struggle at the job site. As some early theorists predicted, conflict has become institutionalized; and, instead of polarizing industrial society, it has had a constructive effect on the operations and structure of economic democracies.

Contrary to the expectations of some theorists, cooperative enterprises have not emerged as a means of reducing conflict and enhancing the interests of all concerned in the production of goods. While some consumers' cooperatives do exist, producers' cooperatives have proved unable to compete with private industry; and, more seriously, their advocates have failed to recognize the potential for conflict that exists wherever an authority structure is established, producing managers and managed.

Exclusiveness versus Inclusiveness

The integration of trade union movements into Western societies has been a gradual process. It received its greatest impetus during World Wars I and II when governments were preoccupied with the prevention of labor disputes which would interrupt production and thus hinder the winning of these global hostilities. The larger value norms of society were imposed upon trade unions in exchange for society's acceptance of these organizations and their methods. The ideology of the industrial theorists gave way to the pragmatism of the bargaining table. Solutions to problems were sought and found (though we must recognize that in employment relationships based on authority structures, once one issue of contention is dealt with another arises). The legitimation of conflict in employment relationships became an essential part of the functioning of both the managers of industry and those who were responsible for the actual production of goods.

The organizations composed of these workers came to accept the legitimacy of conflict also, and with this acceptance of the divergent goals of labor and management came a reorientation of trade union programs and ideologies. In their earlier stages, the trade unions had acted in concert with the socialist parties to seek sweeping or total societal reformation; both denied the legitimacy of the power structure upon which the productive processes were based. The relationship between these two wings of the labor movement had been one of interdependence, with one or the other more active as befitted the circumstances facing the labor movement (a pattern emphasized by the Webbs). But once the trade unions accepted the legitimacy of enterprise through their economic program of collective bargaining, a split developed—in practice if not in ideology—between the trade unions and the socialist parties. Separate working-class cultures continued to exist in Western Europe, but the actions of the trade unions were designed to obtain as much as they could from the existing social order, not to change its basic structure. While unions still mouthed the "ism" of total societal transformation, their *modus operandi* became collective bargaining.

As the trade unions found that they could make economic gains through collective bargaining, they also found themselves developing a stake in the societal *status quo*. To the dismay of their more dogmatic allies, the unions assumed a cautious position, hesitating to take actions that would threaten the economic and noneconomic benefits which they had already obtained. Thus the law of gradualism emerged. Everett Kassalow quotes trade union left-wing socialist Fernando Santi, in his retirement address to the Communist-dominated Italian General Federation of Labor in 1965, when he stated that the trade union movement is made up of individuals with differing political philosophies but a common desire to change the conditions under which they work and live.

> This is why I believe that there is an invisible law that governs— whether we want it or not—the activity of the trade union: the law of graduality. The trade union cannot make appointments with history. Political parties can do so and even they only within certain limits. Each day the union must give an account of itself, of its activity. . . . That is why we must avoid sterile impatience, as we must avoid culpable renunciations. I believe in the secure gain of each day; I believe in the necessity of incorporating the workers' gains in the customs, regulations and laws in order that they be safeguarded and become the civil patrimony of the entire national society.[4]

This split between party and union was further accentuated after World War I in Western Europe when socialist or labor parties either came to power or became important parts of left-of-center interparty coalition governments. The parties assumed a more cautious approach in their exercise of political power, and the trade unions waited in vain for the dramatic societal reforms which the ideological socialists had advocated when they were out of power. Tension developed between the trade unions and the party as the latter played a more centrist role in order to attract the support from interests outside the trade unions which it needed to remain in power and win future parliamentary elections. As a result, the trade unions—while still professing socialist ideology—

retreated further into their shelter of economic progress based on collective bargaining in order to win gains for their membership which were not forthcoming from the socialist government. While studies such as those of Goldthorpe et al. indicate that union members still consider themselves part of a political movement, they concurrently endorse the economic program of collective bargaining which their organizations pursue.

This schizoid type of development and action was not a problem in the United States, where the economically oriented trade unions never had an organic tie to a political party. Lacking a broad societal mission, American unions did not have to face the problems of a split personality caused by a developing divergence between economic and political means. American trade unions entering the political arena did so, and still do so, primarily to reinforce their bargaining position vis-à-vis employers.

Collective bargaining is by definition an exclusive process; that is, it is designed to promote the interests of the members of the bargaining unit on whose behalf the negotiations are being conducted. It has a well-defined concern with the job-related interests of the workers involved. This may be called a selfish approach to promoting the interests of the working class. It is not intended to do away with larger societal problems, nor is it intended to reorganize society according to some predesigned program. In spite of the assertion of the Webbs and others that the political route is more effective than the economic in insuring benefits for the working class, the experience under collective bargaining has proved the contrary. The inroads into management's prerogatives in the daily functioning of a private or public enterprise made by the exclusive means of collective bargaining have not been matched by the political achievements of trade union movements seeking broader societal reform.

The lesson of the effectiveness of collective bargaining has not been lost on Western European trade unionists. While many of the benefits included in collectively negotiated agreements in the United States are legislated in Western Europe, this has not led to a discarding of collective bargaining on the part of Western European unions. While their bargaining program is narrower in scope than is the case in the United States, they continue to use such economic action as the major method to obtain on-the-job benefits for their membership.

Certainly the ideology of Western European trade unions is broader than that of their American counterparts, but even in Western Europe, the dogmatism which formerly existed (perhaps only in theory) is disappearing. The use of collective bargaining has forced these ideological trade unions to be more pragmatic and to concern themselves disproportionately with the concerns of their membership. Gains made via collective bargaining are reflected in the portions of the economy where workers are not protected by collectively negotiated agreements. Such benefits may be passed on to the unorganized workers through legislation by a "friendly" government or through the legally established system of the extension of agreements; or they may be initiated by employers who hope to prevent union organization. Nevertheless, this does not alter the fact that collective bargaining is exclusive, not inclusive, in nature.

Collective bargaining's exclusivity has several side effects. First, it creates unions which become financially independent of any outside organization. A union which engages in collective bargaining and is supported by members' dues gains a degree of autonomy that further reinforces the concept of exclusivity. Such a trade union is able to exert pressure on the polity without any organic connection to a particular political party. Even when such a connection continues to exist, trade unions are able to act independently of the party because of the economic power base which they have developed. The experience in Western Europe demonstrates both the inevitable rise of exclusivity from collective bargaining and the corresponding development of trade union autonomy. While the American trade union movement is closely identified with the Democratic Party, it nevertheless acts as an autonomous organization in a pluralistic democracy. Autonomy and pluralism go hand in hand, and the exclusive process of collective bargaining makes this autonomy possible.

It must be emphasized that this exclusiveness does not mean that unions are politically inert. It does mean that trade unions are able to influence legislation for the public good independent of any specific political party, and they in fact do so. Union autonomy further reinforces the existence of a pluralistic democracy in which unions become an independent political power base operating along with other groups motivated by self-interest. They have ceased to be part of an all-encompassing political movement. It is doubtful that the cautious approach of collective bargaining, with the corresponding exclusivity and trade union autonomy, will ever allow unions to be dominated by any outside organization, including a political party.

Postindustrial Society and the Labor Force[5]

Postindustrialism creates an environment in which the applicability of the industrial theories of the labor movement is laid open to question. The circumstances surrounding trade union activity in postindustrial society differ dramatically from those that existed during the formation of unions in the era of the industrial revolution. The changes in the structure of the economy and the technology required to run a postindustrial society have created differences in the composition of the labor force, and consequently in the structure and function of the trade union movement. Likewise, certain basic assumptions made by the early theorists either were unjustified in the first place or have become irrelevant. This is particularly true of assumptions concerning the role of industrial conflict and of trade unions as conflict organizations.

While predictions and conclusions reached by the Bureau of Labor Statistics of the U.S. Department of Labor in *The U.S. Economy in 1980* must, of course, be considered somewhat speculative in nature, they are based on the best data available for the purpose. These projections were based, however, on eight specific assumptions regarding the state of the world in 1980. (1) First, the Bureau assumed an improvement in the international climate and a corresponding decrease in the strength of the armed forces of the United States. (2) It does not allow for any radical alterations in the "institutional framework" of the economy. (3) It assumes the continuation of present trends in the value placed on work, education, income, and leisure, and (4) the corresponding continuation of economic, social, technological, and scientific trends. (5) For the sake of societal stability, a balance will be struck between low unemployment and "relative price stability" without reducing economic growth. (6) While the activities of all levels of government will expand, the primary expansion will occur at the local and state levels, causing the Congress to direct more funds in that direction. (7) No reduction in the rate of economic development will result from efforts to deal with air pollution and to provide adequate waste disposal. (8) Finally, fertility rates will show a greater decline than has been the case in the past.

Predicting a labor force of 100,000,000 persons in 1980, the Bureau of Labor Statistics sees productivity gains for farm enterprises increasing, and nonfarm productivity advancing at a steady rate, although this will vary according to industry. Government productivity will remain relatively constant, though measurement is difficult because of the predicted substantial increase in government employment (pp. 4–6).

The American economy is the only one in the world, according to theorists such as Daniel Bell, which has already, or will soon, become postindustrial in structure and function. Significant technological change will accompany the evolution of the United States into postindustrialism. The number of computers in use will have doubled during the 1970s, and improvements in productive machinery which *"do not involve drastic departures from conventional design"* will be an important factor in increasing the productivity of certain types of industry. Improvements in the speed and quality of communications will emerge as an important and necessary factor in the evolution of the American economy, as will innovations in the fields of energy and power sources. The Bureau of Labor Statistics also predicts improvements in long-distance transportation, and productivity in construction will increase as the result of changes such as modularization and improvements in basic techniques. Health services will benefit directly from the use of electronic devices such as the computer, and mechanization will be rapid in the harvesting of agricultural food crops.

Improved technology makes possible improvements in productivity. As is the case with economic growth, increases in the rate of productivity will vary from industry to industry and from firm to firm, since technological innovations do not occur simultaneously throughout an industry. However, in all too many cases, technological improvements which result in increases in output cause only small increases in the rate of employment. Growth in employment is also checked by multinational firms' producing goods in foreign countries for sale in American markets. It must also be remembered that the service and government sectors of the economy, which will see the greatest growth rates, are not significantly affected by technological change, and these are the two sectors of a postindustrial economy which will undergo the greatest proportional growth rate and corresponding increase in employment.

The human resources requirements of the American economy are also undergoing drastic alterations concurrently with the changes in economic growth and technological advance. In the largest of all the service industries—wholesale and retail trade—the relative share of total employment in the economy is expected to remain constant, while the proportional rate of employment in transportation, communications, and public utilities will suffer a slight decline. Employment in finance, insurance, and real estate is expected to grow at a rate comparable to that in the past. In the "heterogeneous group of service industries, which include personal, business, health and educational services," there will be a substantial growth in employment largely because of the demand created by rising income. The growth rate

> in business services is expected to be particularly rapid as firms rely increasingly on advertising services to sell their products; on accounting, auditing, bookkeeping, and computing services to handle their recordkeeping; on contract firms to provide maintenance service; and on audit bureaus and collecting agencies to cope with mushrooming consumer credit. (p. 19)

Employment has grown faster in government than in any other sector of the economy, at two and one-half times the rate of increase in total employment. While growth at the federal level will increase only slightly, the level of employment at the local and state levels will continue to expand rapidly. In goods-producing industries, there will be a further decline in agricultural employment, and manpower requirements in manufacturing will increase but at a slower pace. Although one might have expected improved technology to cause decreased employment in the construction industry, technological developments and increased governmental demand will in fact cause a rise in employment.

Occupational Employment[6]

The most significant development in employment will occur in the area of the occupational structure of the labor force. While advances in technology have a direct effect on productivity, which in turn has an indirect effect on employment growth, there is a comparable change in the structure of the labor force as new occupations emerge, others expand, and some contract. A change in the skill requirements of jobs is also created by "revised work rules, new directions in governmental policy, and severe shortages that force substitutions in the kinds of workers hired" (p. 21).

This dramatic change will occur in the tertiary sector of the economy. White-collar occupations have grown faster than blue-collar occupations since 1920, and they will continue to do so. White-collar workers will comprise over half the labor force by 1980, and blue-collar jobs will account for slightly less than one-third of total employment. The remainder of the work force will be employed in service occupations.

The employment growth rate among professional and technical workers "has outdistanced that in all other major occupational groups in recent decades," and this trend will continue. Increases in business and personal incomes along with population growth have increased the demand for these highly trained workers employed in providing goods and services. Increased urbanization has added to this trend. In contrast, the percentage of total employment made up by "managers, officials, and proprietors" will continue at a rate of about 10 percent.

Clerical employment is expected to grow much more rapidly than total employment, although somewhat more slowly than in the 1960s. The major cause of this growth is the expansion taking place in industries that employ sizable clerical staffs. The expected increase in the demand for sales personnel may be held back by the development of new techniques in merchandising. While the number of skilled workers will expand at a slower rate than total employment, the growth in the employment of semiskilled workers will reverse past trends and increase slowly. Semiskilled positions employ more individuals than any other category, and their numbers increased as mass production industry grew. The large growth of industrial unionism, making it and craft unionism the two dominant forces in the American trade union movement, accompanied this development. But technological advances in these mass-production industries will cause the employment of their semiskilled operatives to decline, with severe repercussions for organized labor. By way of contrast, the growth in service employment will enjoy an increase because of underlying societal factors such as population growth, expanded business activity, increased leisure, and higher personal incomes.

The trend which has been obvious in recent years will continue. Economic expansion will create an abundance of positions that will attract greater numbers of young people, university graduates, and women. While the huge increase of teenagers seeking employment will not continue, the major increase in the labor supply will consist of about 34 million young individuals seeking their first jobs. There will be a significant rise in the number of "early career workers" (ages 25–34) in the labor force, but the number of "midcareer" workers (35–44) will decrease slightly. This will coincide with a higher labor force participation rate among women and blacks.

The educational level of the labor force will be higher than ever before. With an increase in the supply of highly educated workers, employers may be likely to prefer these individuals, thus worsening the outlook for the disadvantaged who have limited schooling. While the educational requirements for the white-collar jobs that comprise the majority of the labor force vary according to occupation, the impression may develop that these positions are solely for highly educated individuals. In fact, reserving white-collar jobs for those with higher levels of education may only result in greater frustration and dissatisfaction, since these workers have higher degrees of aspiration than the less educated job seekers and holders. This frustration may result in an inclination toward the only remedy available to these individuals—collective action through a union.

The major source of highly educated and highly trained workers is the country's colleges and universities, and the number of such individuals will increase. The demand for these workers stems from two sources: the growth in employment in certain occupations and the necessity of replacing workers who have left the labor force by attrition. "But another factor is relevant in considering the need for college educated manpower: rising job entry requirements that make a college degree necessary for jobs once performed by workers with lower educational attainment" (p. 35).

Demographic changes in the labor force will force organized labor to face the challenge of a restructured internal membership and the restructuring of appeals to the unorganized. The larger numbers of younger workers with higher levels of educational attainment, the increased labor force participation rate of women, the increase in the number and percentage of black workers in the labor force, and the pressures this will create for the experienced, more mature worker facing the challenge of these three groups all call for a reassessment of structure, role, and function on the part of the trade unions. The divergent, parochial interests of younger workers swelling the ranks of organized labor differ from those of older, more established union members. The struggle between those seeking to emphasize earnings instead of job security, seniority, and pensions will result in internal strife. The new breed of worker/union member may be more interested in obtaining some personal satisfaction from his work than the older worker who views work as a means to an end. Accompanying these types of intraunion problems are interunion problems as changing occupational structures blur jurisdictional boundaries. In addition, there is the problem of attracting the increasing numbers of workers in occupational categories which have been resistant to unionism, as have the types of individuals employed in these expanding (in numbers and proportion) positions.

A Model of Postindustrial Trade Unionism

The inappropriateness of the industrial theories of the trade union movement is an understandable result of the changed environment of postindustrial society. It should be noted that contemporary theorists of trade union structure and function have also failed to take into account the emergence of postindustrialism and the drastic changes that would accompany it. While it must again be emphasized that all ideas are products of the environment in which they are formulated, this does not alter the fact that certain basic assumptions upon which industrial theories are based are no longer valid. A brief acquaintance with the developments since the advent of the industrial revolution must invariably lead one to doubt the viability of the explanations that have been discussed thus far.

The development of postcapitalistic society presents the first challenge to the appropriateness of these works. The degree of governmental regulation and intervention in the economy and in society generally was not foreseen by the industrial theorists. Likewise, the consequences of the evolution from industrial to postindustrial economies and societies was not taken into account by the majority of latter-day theorists. The changes in technology, the makeup of the labor force, the creation of new societal power centers, and the institutionalization of the conflict inherent in all employment relationships call for attempts to rethink the role of postindustrial trade unions. This discussion is meant to be "an" explanation of trade union structure and function in postindustrial society; no dogmatic pretence is made for its being "the" explanation.

Trade unions which have organized the "old" labor force will continue to exist in postindustrial society. Although the proportion of workers who have traditionally been the most prone to organize and have served as the core of the American trade union movement will comprise a smaller percentage of the total labor force, their presence will continue to be felt both economically and politically. These unions will maintain their focus and emphasis on the use of collective bargaining to protect the job rights of their members and to ensure as high an economic reward as is possible for the workers they represent. At the same time, they are likely to engage in experiments to meet their changed environment. Alternatives to traditionally accepted trade union functions will be developed as circumstances call for them.

While the majority of traditional trade unions will continue to be defensive in character, protecting their membership from the challenges of technological change, the rise of the multinational corporation, and competition from abroad, history demands that they demonstrate the flexibility to deal with these problems through negotiations and lobbying for legislative action. Certainly evidence of this adjustment already exists. The expansion of trade unionism in the public sector, the efforts at coordinated bargaining among unions both within and outside of the AFL-CIO, the use of interest arbitration as a substitute for the strike by unions such as the United Steelworkers of America, and the never-ending drive to organize the unorganized are illustrative of this new flexibility.

Past trends indicate that organized labor will continue to exercise an economic, political, and societal influence far beyond what one might expect from a mere glance at the total number of organized workers. The far-reaching influence of organized labor is made possible by its economically based organizational structure. This organization, held together by the common interests of its members in economic and political factors affecting their working and off-the-job lives, provides a ready-made structure that has been and will be mobilized in campaigns to protect and promote the interests of both active and inactive union membership. The power of this organizational structure will continue to be used in attempts to push American society in directions felt to be specifically to the advantage of union members. Organized labor will also continue to make its presence felt on broader social issues.

Unions are inherently democratic organizations. While it is true that the leadership of any organization will try to perpetuate itself in office, unions have not suffered from the existence of internal autocratic machines to anywhere near the extent predicted by those who took a dismal view of the prospects for trade union democracy. While autocracy does of course exist in some unions, the nature of trade unions as conflict organizations breeds a contempt for monolithic internal structures and creates activists ready to challenge the existing union leadership, although not always successfully.

While it varies from union to union, enough turnover of union leadership has occurred at all levels of a trade union hierarchy to lend credence to this contention. Mechanisms for internal control are built into unions as they are into all viable organizations in American society, but they have not been constructed to stifle legitimate internal dissention. Internal controls are vital if a union is to confront employers as a collectivity, lobby successfully politically, fulfill its obligations to construct collective agreements, and prevent disintegrating forces from reducing the organization to sheer anarchy. It must be kept in mind that collective bargaining is possible only if employers are able to deal with an organization which can be truly held accountable for the actions of its membership.

The serious challenge facing organized labor is not the threat of institutional aging or the domination of "union bosses." It must be recognized that the creation of a formalized organizational structure makes collective bargaining work, and it is a necessary corollary to the institutionalization of conflict arising in employment situations. It must further be remembered that power in our society no longer rests with individuals. While persons who have accumulated or inherited great amounts of economic wealth are able to exert a societal influence which cannot be matched to any degree by the ordinary citizen, an employee can attempt to counter such influence by collective organization on the job and thereby develop an economic power base of his own. Even self-employed individuals have learned this lesson and have formed associations to represent their interests.

The basic difference which exists between interest groups is whether they are designed to pursue, in a general way, the interests of a specific type or group of individuals, or whether they are single-issue organizations. Single-issue groups often lose their *raison d'être* once their one specific goal has been reached. Although it must be admitted that some such groups demonstrate flexibility and change their goals, a dilemma which faces utopian trade union movements is that they may cease to have a societal function once their particular version of utopia is achieved. Nevertheless, Sidney and Beatrice Webb claimed that trade unions had no less significant a role to play under socialism than under capitalism. In any case, the pragmatic American trade union movement has never had to face this problem.

Trade unions in postindustrial society can be understood only within the context of organizations whose primary purpose is to protect and pursue the job-related interests of their membership. This is the core of unionism, the cement that holds the organization together. The key to trade union existence in postindustrial society is the development of workers' common job-related interests into a viable organizational structure. In the postindustrial era, the "new" worker who emerges from the restructuring of the labor force will be attracted to organizations whose primary concern surrounds the work situation. These highly educated professional and technical workers, along with their less-trained white-collar, service, and clerical employee counterparts, will feel powerless as individuals facing an established authority structure. The pragmatic nature of the employee in America is not dead. History will repeat itself, and workers will form and join organizations to gain collectively what they are unable to obtain individually, seeking goals directly related to their employment situations.

While their aims will be specific at a given time, this specificity will dissolve once each issue is resolved. Essential to the functioning of these organizations is the recognition that successful trade union action consists of seeking resolutions to problems, not ultimate solutions which allegedly will keep an issue from rising again. Thus they will seek in a general way to service the job-related needs and aspirations of their membership. These needs will of course differ from those of industrial workers, and they will involve a wider range of items. In bargaining on behalf of professional or technical employees, much more is negotiable than is the case when the employees have less education, training, expertise, and job autonomy. While a worker plays many different roles in American society, his concern with job-related issues transcends his other concerns. The heterogeneity of the American work force will continue to exist in postindustrial society. The commonality of interests in the employment situation, which is a necessary element in an individual's other social roles, is obvious enough to draw together workers of differing ideologies and philosophies. The individual's *Weltanschauung* yields to the pragmatic concerns surrounding his employment.

The fulfillment of this essential trade union function forms a base of economic power which solidifies the rank and file and allows trade unions to make labor's presence a powerful one in the societal arena. From this same base of economic power comes the ability to make organized labor's influence felt elsewhere—on the economy, on the polity, and on social issues. If one assumes that conflict and flux are realities of society,[7] this definition assumes even greater meaning. The trade union movement is working gradually and progressively toward a postindustrial society in which the power of its membership (in their role as employees) is at least comparable to that of the business community and the government. This primary function is combined with a secondary function which has often been termed "social unionism": the effort to improve the condition of the entire community. In the pursuit of these larger, societal goals unionism may be viewed as a movement with a social philosophy—less specific, less well-defined, and less rigid than the union's primary function, but nonetheless present in postindustrial society. It is the emphasis on the primary function, however, which enables the trade union movement to manifest its resources in support of larger societal programs.*

It is possible to divide the areas in which trade unions will function in postindustrial society into three basic types. The first category consists of matters directly pertaining to the job-related interests of the membership; that is, issues of union/employee vis-à-vis management. Second, the economic power

*Thomas R. Donahue, an assistant to AFL-CIO president George Meany, spelled out this philosophy quite succinctly in a speech to the Washington, D.C., chapter of the Industrial Relations Research Association. See Donahue, in *John Herling's Labor Letter*.

base created by collective bargaining will continue to enable unions to mobilize the rank and file on political issues, using the organizational structure built up around the effective presence of the union on the job site. These issues may be of direct or indirect concern to job-related matters; the motivation may be selfish or altruistic; but in any case it is here that one finds social unionism.

At times, some trade union leaders will venture off into areas which their members view as marginal to their on-the-job interests and needs. Some of these issues will be extremely marginal, and they will be tolerated only as long as a union executive is fulfilling its role as protector and combatant on the job; that is, as long as resources are not diverted from the union's primary task and function. Should a trade union's leadership lose sight of its primary function, one of two possible results will occur: either the leadership will be replaced by a more realistic one, or the union will find its ability to function as a social force decreased, since the erosion of a union's economic power base will inevitably lead to the erosion of societal power.

While trade unions in postindustrial society will play a more aggressive policymaking part in the upper echelons of the societal hierarchy, they will at the same time be engaged in a seemingly contradictory role as agents of job-site militancy, for the struggle for job protection, job rights, and work autonomy is one without end.[8] Conflict arising from employment situations will be institutionalized in postindustrial society just as it was in the past. While the role played by unions in altering the authority structure of the postindustrial job situation will far exceed anything existing in industrial society, job-site militancy will continue to have a conservative political function. The reason is that militancy gives rise to democracy on the job site, and industrial democracy is supportive of political democracy. Through collective bargaining, employees of all types will be given a stake in the *status quo*, and the extent of this vested interest will be greater than was possible in industrial society.

Industrial versus Occupational Unionism

One of the recurring themes in trade union history is the argument between the proponents of craft and of industrial unionism. It is a dispute which fills labor history in the second half

of the nineteenth century, eventually ending with the victory
of craft unionism and the rise of the AFL. The argument for
craft unionism was a strong one, and it met the one critical
test—it succeeded. Such unionism was job conscious, not
class conscious. Its advocates held that only skilled workers
displayed the unity of economic interest which could tie a
union together as a viable organization. Because skilled
workers could not be replaced as easily as unskilled workers,
the early craft unionists sought to establish their power position by controlling the supply of labor.

With the coming of the age of mass production, it became
obvious that the philosophy of unionization according to craft
was incapable of organizing the workers employed in large-
scale industries; yet it was not until the 1930s that the advocates of industrial unionism were able to prove their case.
Advocating one large union for each mass-production industry, these industrial unionists were able to take advantage of
the stagnation of craft unionism, the legislation of the New
Deal, and the unsatiated desire of unskilled and semiskilled
workers in mass production industries for the protection from
the unilateral power of industrial management which collective organization could provide. Vertically structured unionism, organizing all employees of an employer regardless of
skill or occupation, succeeded where the advocates of horizon-
tal organization by skill or job failed.

The arguments used by the advocates of craft and industrial
unionism are both valid depending on the era in which they
are proffered and the environment in which they find themselves. The existence of several units organized around specific occupations all dealing with a single employer (or several
employers) allows for a whipsawing effect; given different ex-
piration dates, one unit's contract negotiators could use the
previously bargained contract of another unit as a floor from
which to begin. This would give added leverage to a union's
bargaining position. Taking into account the degree of skill
that the workers in a specific unit might have and the essentiality of that unit's operation in a productive process, the
structure of occupational organization might put a unit (or
units) in a strategic position if the operations of an employer
were to continue. If such a unit went on strike, the entire
operation of an employer would have to shut down. This type
of strategically located unit could set a pattern that other less
powerful units could follow.

Countering that point of view is the contention that a multiplicity of bargaining units weakens the bargaining power of the workers involved. Allowing one large employer (or group of employers) to deal with several small units places all the aces in the employer's hand. A strike by a small number of workers could not shut down a large enterprise; especially in the absence of a strategically placed unit, an employer would thus be in a dominant bargaining position. Lack of numbers might even enable an employer to break such a unit and put an end to collective bargaining. Even with the existence of a strategically placed craft unit, there is no guarantee that the benefits derived from an agreement negotiated by such a unit would be spread throughout a firm or industry. In fact, the existence of a large number of relatively small bargaining units allows an employer to play one unit off against another.

One large unit consisting of all the employees of an employer, group of employers, or industry has bargaining strength based on the massive number of workers organized. Such a unit is able to present a united front against an employer, which is impossible under occupational organization. Such large industrial units also lend themselves more easily to the coordinated bargaining efforts of several unions facing a group of employers, a multi-industry employer, or a multinational employer. The problems created by the divisiveness of occupational organization are nonexistent in industrial or wall-to-wall organization.

The relative effectiveness of these two forms of trade union organization must be weighed under the circumstances created by a postindustrial society. The composition of the labor force is critical here. Under postindustrialism, the labor force is tertiary, predominantly white collar, service oriented, younger, and highly educated. The number and proportion of "traditional" union members and unionized enterprises shrinks in the evolution into postindustrialism. In viewing trade unionism in postindustrial society, some theorists advocate the creation of industrial or vertical unionism, joining together professional, white collar, service, clerical, skilled, semiskilled, and unskilled employees. It is asserted that this form of organization is the only one capable of forcing decisive changes upon employers; that only vertical organization is able to challenge the very basis of the decision-making power emanating from the authority structure of an enterprise; and that this organizational form will have societal ramifications beyond the bargaining table and the work situation, affecting the very basis of organized society.

However, it is necessary to investigate the appeal which such an organizational structure will have upon the largely unorganized new working force. The drive for a new labor movement will not be led by organizations of employees in the secondary sector of a dual labor market. The advantage that these workers derive from the strength of their numbers alone is offset by the weak bargaining position resulting from their easy replacability. The typical employing unit in postindustrial society will be small in comparison to the large mass-production units of industrial society. The shutting down of one employer or even a group of employers by such vertically organized workers at the bottom of the employment totem pole will not dramatically affect the performance of a particular service; an employer has too many alternate sources of labor power available. This is true in spite of the fact that in a service-oriented enterprise income lost through a strike cannot be regained; customers and consumers have too many alternative sources to go to for a needed service. Only in goods-producing firms can lost production be made up once the employees go back to work, provided that customers return once production resumes.

Doubt must also be cast on the effectiveness of an appeal for vertical organization among the unorganized. American workers have clearly demonstrated a proclivity for taking collective action to protect and pursue their job-related interests. They have not typically joined or formed trade unions to transform the basic structure of society, the economy, or the polity. Successful trade unionism is based upon fulfilling the economic and noneconomic needs perceived by employees as arising from their work situations. Call it greed, selfishness, or the result of the overall economic/pragmatic nature of American institutions; the fact is that appeals directed at the interests of employees in the name of economic gains and security, job equity and dignity, and the derivation of satisfaction and self-gratification from the work or employment process will succeed in postindustrial society, and appeals to altruism will likely fail.

Given the dictates of the newly reconstructed labor force in postindustrial society, these appeals to the interests of workers will take the form of filling the voids created by new occupations. The sense of identification which these professional, technical, service, and clerical employees have will center on their occupation first, and only secondly on the type of enterprise which employs them. The authors of *Industrialism and Industrial Man* will prove correct in their assumption that an employee's reference group will be his occupation. While vertical organization may be the only way to organize those in the lower echelons of the white-collar and service hierarchy and those lacking the skills and education needed for employment in postindustrial society, the major form of organizational appeal which will succeed in uniting the majority of the new labor force for the purpose of collective action must be directed at the work-related interests and problems of these individuals.

Such organizations will find themselves able to develop an economic power base which can serve to counteract the power of employers, the government, and other organized groups in postindustrial society. These new workers will discover that Samuel Gompers was correct when he said that from economic power comes all other forms of societal power. And the most effective way for them to develop an economic power base is to form collective bargaining organizations based around their occupational concerns. These common concerns will supersede the workers' non–job-related interests and the societal roles they play.

The organizational structure of future trade union federations may come to resemble those of Sweden, where there are three separate labor confederations: one of blue-collar manufacturing employees; one of technical white-collar employees; and one of professional employees who tend to be university graduates. Another possibility is that vertical trade unions will continue to exist, but they will be broken down into sections based on occupation as are the general unions of Western Europe. If this occurs, internal organizational power will tend to reside disproportionately in the occupational divisions made up of those workers at the top of the employment hierarchy—the highly educated professional and technical employees.

These occupationally structured organizations will not altogether resemble the craft unions of the industrial era. They will engage in practices to maintain their occupational status and will develop vested interests in entrance to the occupation; but they will also be more aggressive rather than merely reacting to changes in the employment environment. They may even use collective bargaining to establish their status as professionals or workers entitled to exercise a great deal of personal autonomy on the job. From such aggressive actions may come the drive for work satisfaction. These new labor organizations will consist of members who are not content to consider work only as the price they have to pay for a higher standard of living. The job-related issue of humanizing the work process and developing of individual responsibility will be of paramount importance in holding these organizations together. It will be the postindustrial counterpart of the preservation of the craft prerogatives of the industrial era.

These changes indicate that occupational organization will give rise to a new form of trade union militancy, much more offensive than defensive in character. The highly qualified workers in these organizations will be less likely to blindly accept preexisting authority structures. They will serve as the core of a new labor movement, more given to experimentation and innovation than their industrial counterparts. Such workers will choose to be led by a new, more militant brand of trade union leader. The institutional aging predicted by Lester will be far less prevalent in these new organizations—which may not be "new" in the sense of first being established in the postindustrial era. Existing trade unions may take up the challenge of organizing these "new" workers, and in so doing they will find themselves in the vanguard of a new, militant labor movement. Benefits they obtain will drift downward throughout the rest of the employing enterprise and the labor force. Their example will be emulated by workers capable of such action; and those organizations composed of workers unable to exert similar bargaining power will also benefit from this downward drift, but will continue to resemble the more defensive trade unions of the past.

5

The Effect of Affluence

Both the Westleys and Mark van de Vall describe the emergence of a new type of worker, trade union member, and union organization as the direct result of the widespread dispersion of the benefits of economic growth and prosperity. It must be remembered that both claims—that a new breed of worker is emerging and that unions have a different role to play in the era of the welfare state—arose from the economic growth of the 1950s and 1960s, and that the economic environment has altered considerably since these two contentions were put forward. Nonetheless, these concepts must be taken into consideration in any attempt to analyze the internal and external functioning of trade unions in modern society. While neither the Westleys nor van de Vall deal with the evolution of a postindustrial society, they raise questions that are applicable to postindustrialism.

Data available from the Bureau of Labor Statistics support the Westleys' contention that younger and more highly educated workers are becoming more prevalent in the evolution into postindustrialism. The Westleys hold that this "emerging worker" will be less likely to accept preexisting authority structures either in his employment or within the trade union which represents him at the bargaining table and on the job. Authors other than the Westleys, Daniel Bell, and Mark van de Vall have forecast a resulting decline in trade union strength, membership, and effectiveness.[1] Citing the inability of unions to organize the white-collar workers who comprise an ever-growing proportion of the labor force, the lack of organization among highly trained technical workers, and the negative effects of technological change in industry, they claim that the strength of trade unions has reached a plateau.[2]

Opposing trends are, however, noted. Unlike the relatively homogeneous force of industrial workers in the early stages of the industrial revolution, the work force required by modern industrial society is heterogeneous, and the union is said to play a significant role in the operation of the industrial system. "By helping to frame the rules and by participating in their administration through the grievance machinery, the union serves invaluably to mitigate the feeling that such systems or their administration are arbitrary or unjust."[3] In the absence of such bilaterally administered grievance systems, a realistic management is forced to develop comparable mechanisms to channel worker protest.

It should also be noted that not every trade union has adopted the position of being unalterably opposed to technological change as a threat to its members' jobs and the organization's power position. Some union leaders have recognized the inevitability of technological change, and in so doing, have assisted industrial management in softening its effects on the work force. Indeed, where possible, they have made it work to the advantage of their membership by means of trade-offs in which higher rates of pay, shorter work weeks, or provisions for early retirement are the *quid* for the *quo* of technological change. While such measures may help to deal with the problems which changes create for a specific union or a particular enterprise, they do nothing to affect its wider societal repercussions.

Some individuals assume a more cautious approach in describing the psychological makeup of the "new" workers and their influence on the organizations that represent (or attempt to represent) them. In one such study, John H. Goldthorpe and his associates concentrated on the role of affluence in the totality of a worker's existence, not just in his work relationships. Granted that their survey research was conducted in a country (Great Britain) where the trade union movement has traditionally been much more class conscious than is the case in the United States; nonetheless, their conclusions are relevant in evaluating the effect of affluence upon the American worker and his union.

Goldthorpe and his associates did not discover any drastic alteration in the mental makeup of the affluent worker in British society. They agree with the contention in Chapter 4 of this book that the worker's main concern with his union is that organization's economic role as a representative or combatant on the job site.

In addition, affluent workers were found to have a truncated value system in which the economic and political functions of a trade union were viewed as being cut off from one another; that is, a distinction has emerged between the economic conflict via-à-vis management and the broader political conflicts which take place in society.

This distinction between conflict surrounding an employment relationship and political conflict puts the former into proper perspective when the government is the employer. In a nationalized industry or enterprise, conflict between the workers and their union and those in positions of management is not identified as conflict between trade unions and the government. A strike against such a nationalized industry or firm is not a political strike. Although such strike activity may in fact be used to protest some broader stand or policy position taken by a ruling government, it is more directly the result of the conflict inherent in all employment relationships.

Apparently, union action taken by these "new" workers is directed against those who have authority over them. As the composition of the labor force changes with the evolution into postindustrial society, the more highly educated younger worker will use his union as a protest mechanism at the limited level of job-related matters and not as a means to achieve broad societal change. If societal repercussions result from job-related actions, so much the better; to achieve these broader concerns is not the primary function of trade unions in postindustrial society.

Predictions based on the emergence of a "new" type of worker have been contradicted by many recent developments, and must further be called into question because of the evolution into a postindustrial society, with all its implications. The emphasis that has been placed on the repercussions of spreading affluence has failed to take into account the diversity of the postindustrial labor force. The nature of the emerging worker's employment situation will dictate that the worker's reaction to an extent that cannot be explained away solely by the expansion of "affluence" to a greater proportion of a country's population.

While they will comprise at most only about one-third of the total labor force, blue-collar mass-production jobs will continue to exist. These types of occupations most readily lend themselves to mechanization, automation, and technological advances in general. Since they can be broken down into a number of minuscule human actions, they tend to be the most repetitive and therefore the most boring. It is doubtful that the desire for "meaningful" work can be accomplished when a machine is used to govern and pace human activity. There are some jobs whose very nature prevents any real built-in interest or satisfaction; and one of the "new breed" employed in such a position will most likely find himself just as dead-ended as the more traditional worker. The emerging worker, then, will probably be in the forefront of the discontented in jobs controlled by mass-production techniques.

The ultimate fractionalization of mass-production jobs takes place when automation techniques are applied to these functions; productive processes are then initiated by machines which also perform the function of quality control. This system may, however, have a different psychological effect. In fact, the argument has been made that workers employed in automated enterprises hold a set of values and job expectations comparable to those of the highly skilled worker of the industrial and preindustrial era. In his study of workers employed in the continuous-flow automated production system of the chemical industry, Robert Blauner[4] suggested that a continuous-process type of technology "contains tendencies toward greater interest and involvement and toward greater monotony and boredom";[5] the former tendencies, Blauner claimed, are greater than the latter. Something in such a form of automated technology seems to create work involvement even if the worker possesses little by way of skill or training and is nothing more than a mere operative in the productive process. Responsibility and the chance for "growth and development" help to fill the void and erase the tendency toward boredom which one might expect to find plaguing a worker in an otherwise powerless position. As is the case with the blue-collar operative in mass production industry, the chemical worker tends to identify with the firm which employs him; but unlike the mass production worker, he does so in a positive way.

In addition to the relative off-the-job affluence which allows him to enjoy a higher standard of living, the new worker may find built-in factors which provide for fulfillment in an automated job: job security, the existence of career patterns, a diversified job structure, responsibility and variety, self-determination of time responsibilities and movement, and the integration of the work force into "a cohesive industrial community."[6] If such conditions are present in an automated facility, it is likely that its workers will be resistant to the appeals of unionization (though they may also feel that they are dominated by the job's technology).

On the other hand, if automation and other improvements in postindustrial technology cause a loss of control over the job, or make any real control impossible, the workers employed in the affected positions will be likely to resort to collective action. Again assuming a more highly educated and younger postindustrial labor force, jobs at the bottom of the white-collar and service hierarchy, such as clerical and sales positions, may be susceptible to a degree of control by management which was not possible in industrial society. These individuals, who have traditionally been at great pains to establish a status difference between themselves and the blue-collar work force, may find themselves just as powerless as the mass-production worker. Unlike the highly educated portion of the labor force, they will turn toward trade unionism in an attempt to regain what technological change has caused them to lose. Their organizations will resemble the defensive type of unionism generally associated with the assembly-line worker in industrial society.

Again we will find a category of worker organizing on the basis of common concerns related to a work position. It is questionable whether off-the-job affluence will take the place of their need for dignity, job control, job equity, and job satisfaction. Their education—though less extensive or intensive than that of professional and technical employees—has caused them to develop aspirations that will not be met in the jobs in which they find themselves employed. Given the adaptive nature of trade unionism, it is only a matter of time before these employees make use of their collective power to countervail the unilateral power of their employers.

Even in the presence of the welfare state which van de Vall describes, the primary function of such workers' organizations will be to meet the job-related needs of their membership. Any attempt to place the needs of the membership second to a larger societal goal will result in the death of the union that tries to do so, or its replacement by an organization which is more in touch with the realities of employment relationships.

Likewise, off-the-job affluence will not override the on-the-job needs and aspirations of highly skilled professional and technical workers. While organizations of these types of employees will, as has been previously stated, tend to be more aggressive/offensive and demonstrate a greater willingness and ability to adapt to the changed and changing surroundings in which their members find themselves employed, trade unions will be able to sell themselves to such employees only by stressing job-related issues and occupational concerns. These employees at the top of the employment hierarchy will be less likely than any others to accept the terms and conditions of employment dictated to them by their employers. Their education and training will give them a high degree of ability and sophistication. Indeed, they will know more about the requirements of their occupation than do those who supervise and/or employ them. They will use collective bargaining to establish or reinforce the talent which they bring to the job and to develop a degree of autonomy far exceeding anything their less trained and educated fellow unionists could even hope for. Such workers are more likely to take off-the-job affluence as given. While direct economic matters will of course be of paramount importance to these employees—especially when they compare their economic status to that of less trained and educated workers—they will demand a degree of responsibility, authority, and autonomy on the job which will make them unique, the elite of the new trade union movement.

Thus what one might call a two-pronged nonmanualist psychology will develop among the white-collar service-oriented or tertiary sector of the economy which will comprise two-thirds of the total labor force. The first will more closely resemble the defensive protectionist union of industrial society. The second, while it will demonstrate some degree of protectionism, will consist of the new breed of optimistic, aggressive/offensive technical and professional employees. The structure and function of the trade unions organized by both categories of workers will depend upon the relationship of these workers to their jobs, and they will emerge in spite of any degree of affluence—which is of course a relative term to begin with—that might exist.

Authority in Employment Relationships

A discussion of the role of affluence, or relative affluence, in postindustrial society and its effect upon both trade unions and their present and potential members would be incomplete without taking into consideration the one feature common to all employment relationships—the authority structure required to operate a goods-producing firm or a service-providing enterprise.

This internal authority or power structure is inherent to all employing enterprises—that is, almost all businesses that consist of more than one person. If an enterprise is to provide the intended goods or services, some sort of internal structure has to be devised, either consciously or unconsciously. This structure creates differentiated internal positions. To invoke a term which has been used on several occasions previously, a web of rules is developed to describe the authority, responsibility, and rights of every individual within the organizational hierarchy. As the positions of superiors and subordinates are created, the function and power of these two different but equally necessary positions causes a divergence of interests to emerge. The individuals who find themselves in these positions of domination or subjection develop parochial interests which may differ from the broader and major concerns of the enterprise: to provide a maximum of goods or services of a particular quality at the lowest possible cost; that is, a maximum of income over outlay.

The very nature of the enterprise therefore lends itself to the formation of informal interest groups within its formalized structure. These interest groups are created in an attempt to meet the needs and desires of a particular group of individuals who cannot obtain their goals through the official organization or on an individual basis. These groups include employees of all types, but they are most likely to be formed by those lacking in authority, be they staff personnel or those in subordinate positions. The existence of such informal interest groups may work counter to the goals of the managers who control the enterprise, in which case they pose a serious problem for management. Many managers are aware of this situation and attempt to alleviate or suppress it, but too often they deal with the symptoms, not the causes, of the problem.

The natural reaction of any person or group whose authority is challenged, including enterprise managers and management, is to resist such a threat to their unilateral power to make decisions affecting others. This managerial rejection of the informal employee community is usually enough to convince the employees that their only hope is to resort to formalized measures. These measures—union organization and collective bargaining—have added attractiveness for employees because they can be enforced by federal, and often state, legislation.

Employees therefore react in an organized, collective manner; and while some employers are in fact able to blunt such efforts by resorting to a series of legal, illegal, and semilegal acts, they are unable to do away with the independent variable which creates what for them is a problem: they cannot do away with the authority structure. Employing enterprises cannot be run like a town meeting if their objectives are to be achieved. The existence of conflict in employment situations cannot be dismissed as mere friction, as some theorists would have us believe. It is inherent to all employment situations and universal in nature.

Peter Drucker viewed the basic conflict between those in authority (the managers) and those subject to that authority (the managed) as resulting from the fact that the employing enterprise views wages as a cost item, and the employees view monetary rewards as income. A management assuming this attitude may merely try to assume the burden of additional costs by buying off the employees involved in the formation of these informal interest groups. While this may mollify employees temporarily, it still deals only with the symptoms of the problem, not the cause.

The problem, however, is not as simple as Drucker would have us believe; its cause is to be found in the authority structure of the enterprise. To put it bluntly, the needs and aspirations of all employees subject to unilateral authority—specifically economic rewards and security, equity on the job, and the derivation of some satisfaction from the work performed—run counter to the tendency, and perhaps the necessity, of management to treat the human element in the enterprise like any other factor of production, as a commodity.

The problem does not lend itself to solutions; the changing nature of enterprise, work environments, and employment relationships in general ensures that as soon as one item of contention is dealt with, another will arise. Those who think that they can produce an absolute harmony of interests throughout an employing enterprise are deluding themselves. Such an attitude may even be self-destructive, for it guarantees that when formalized conflict does erupt it will assume an extreme, uncompromising nature.

The existence of a welfare state or the emergence of an affluent working class does nothing to alter the authority structure inherent in all employment relationships. The newly existent affluence is separate from the work site. It is part of the vast area of a worker's life which is outside the jurisdiction of the trade union as the protector of job-site rights. Thus affluence, or relative affluence, does not make the union member any more placid on the job.

Even if every worker owns a car, a house, and whatever other comforts of civilization there are, the root of industrial class conflict is not only not eliminated, but hardly touched. The fact that economic demands may prove the substance of manifest interests must not give rise to the erroneous notion that satisfaction of these demands eliminates the causes of conflict. Social conflict is as universal as the relations of authority and imperatively coordinated associations, for it is the distribution of authority that provides the basis and cause of its occurrence.[7]

Additionally, the threat of unemployment still belies the cozy picture painted by some postindustrial theorists, especially for those whose positions most closely resemble those of industrial workers. The struggle for equity on the job site is seemingly one without end. This job-site militancy is necessary to maintain and improve the individual worker's off-the-job economic and social status.[8]

This divergence of interests between the order givers and the order takers is even more relevant in postindustrial society than it was in the preindustrial and industrial eras. The postindustrial working class includes a much broader range of employee type than was true in industrial society, due to the altered composition of the labor force and the increased percentage of members of the labor force who are employees. In particular, enterprises in postindustrial society require a greater number and proportion of highly trained and educated employees. It is precisely these employees who are more reluctant to accept judgments from above without question, and less likely to be satisfied with attempts to merely buy them off. They bring a greater degree of expertise to a job than is true of the situation in industrial society, and they therefore expect to have a greater amount of "say" in determining the structure and function of their job. Just as is the case with the skilled, semiskilled, and unskilled employee in both industrial and postindustrial society, the white-collar, service, and clerical workers, who are much more prevalent in postindustrialism, will find a need to protect their own interests on the job because of the authority structure inherent to the employing enterprise. This attitude is equally, or even more widely held by the highly educated technical and professional employee.

Postindustrial society will come to recognize the continued existence and legitimacy of labor-management conflict and the inevitability of trade unionism and collective bargaining as the means of dealing with it. It will also have become accustomed to the occurrence of occasional strikes which result from this conflict.

The wisdom of Western democracies has been demonstrated in their efforts to establish mechanisms to institutionalize the conflict emerging from employment relationships. This creates another parochial interest group in a pluralistic society, and gives a larger number and proportion of the citizenry a stake in the *status quo;* democracy in employment situations reinforces political democracy.

While affluence does nothing to eliminate this authority relationship and the resultant potential for conflict inherent in any employment relationship, it is indicative of the improved economic and social status made possible by the existence of trade unionism and collective bargaining. The broadened range of benefits reflects the flexibility of trade unions in attempting to meet the modern-day changing needs of their membership. A new type of militancy emerges as trade unionism expands throughout the newly structured labor force, but this militancy is much more evident at the level of the job site than at a societal, policy-making level. As was the case in industrial society, there is a conservative nature of job-site militancy which becomes apparent, for while this militancy provides a degree of vitality to an employment relationship which would otherwise be impossible, it allows conflict to be institutionalized in a constructive manner.

The Weakness of Class-Conscious Unionism

The model of trade unionism that has been predicted for a postindustrial society has the primary function of protecting and pursuing the job-related interests of its membership. This approach transcends ideologies and does not formulate any carefully defined ultimate ends. It is concerned with the resolution, not the elimination, of conflict. This problem-oriented type of unionism recognizes that the members will always seek to defend themselves and promote their own parochial interests in the face of a management which seeks to minimize or do away with this job-site control. Thus the struggle is endless, and success breeds success.

While it has been proposed that the bonds of class hold a union together more strongly than any other ties, class-conscious unions, because of their ideological blinders, are unable to achieve as much as unions that focus on job-related issues. They suffer from a schizoid condition as a result of seeking a new social order at the same time that they are, in practice, behaving as wage bargainers. In fact, economic gains (and progress on noneconomic issues) breed failure for unions with ultimate ends. Success in collective bargaining and the presence of affluence or a welfare state tend to destroy the bonds of class which hold a class-conscious trade union movement together, and the ideology of yesteryear wanes as the standard of living improves.

In postindustrial society, trade unions will be occupation- or job-oriented, and will thus be able to unite divergent types of individuals around a readily identifiable set of goals and community of interest. This is essential in dealing with the emerging generation of worker/union member. For this younger and more highly educated individual, the class struggle exists only in history. He is not disposed to make sacrifices for some vague concept of class solidarity that has little real meaning for him. Success or affluence or the presence of a welfare state has broken the bonds which held ideological labor movements together, and the appeals and war cries of the past fall on deaf ears. Thus trade unionism as a way of life seems doomed. The separate working-class societies of the late nineteenth and early twentieth centuries will become nothing but a part of history in a postindustrial society.

The trade union movements of Western Europe will undergo dramatic alterations in structure and function which will not be necessary for the nonideological American unions. Ideologues like Andre Gorz will see their programs for politicizing trade union movements reduced to academic arguments as workers find themselves able to accomplish economically, through the mechanisms of collective negotiations, what they have only been promised by the programmatic socialists. When the nations of Western Europe follow the United States into postindustrialism, the shock waves will be severe for trade unions and trade unionists who have held on to the belief that unions have a function with a "higher calling" to fulfill. The difference between actuality and ideology will broaden, and ideological trade unions will have to seriously rethink their roles and regroup themselves if they are to play an influential role in postindustrial society. They must begin with a reassessment of their role vis-à-vis the polity if they are to survive as viable organizations.

6

Trade Unions and the Polity

Consistent with the evolutionary pattern evident in the past, trade unions have continued to develop along two apparently contradictory paths. The primary direction taken by unions is to seek on-the-job and off-the-job improvements for their membership vis-à-vis employers. At this level of action, trade union militancy is the rule—necessarily so if benefits are to be maximized. Such tactics perform a dual function: (1) They provide cohesiveness for the union as an organization and tend to bind the membership together into a united whole. Militant tendencies and actions in dealing with employers most greatly enhance the economic and noneconomic conditions of a union's membership. This creates a solidarity which can later be used again in the fight to pursue the membership's on-the-job interests. (2) It has already been noted that this type of action creates a viable, autonomous interest group in a pluralistic democracy—one which must be taken into consideration by the polity. These actions thus create a healthy vitality at the job site in a union's daily confrontations with employers, and a comparable political vigor. Where such an independent trade-union movement exists, it is unlikely that a single party or organization will become the focal institution in a society and thus dominate a nation's total existence.

At a separate, perhaps higher, level, an evolutionary process has occurred as the trade unions' primary aim is achieved. Making gains through an established social system gives a trade union movement a vested interest in that system. It is here that we again are able to observe the conservative societal nature of job-site militancy. As labor organizations are increasingly integrated into the existing social order, they are, and in fact must be, given opportunities to participate in basic policy-making and decision-making procedures in the postindustrial state. Union power cannot be ignored by the polity. In dealing with these broader societal issues, trade unions allow the large mass of their membership to participate indirectly with other powerful and autonomous interest groups in society. Whether it be in election campaigns, the lobbying activity which takes place behind the passage of legislation, or actual participation and cooperation with the polity, trade unions have the ability to act as equals with comparable parochial interest groups. Postindustrial trade unions will find themselves increasingly able to walk in the "corridors of power."

There is a natural built-in reluctance on the part of many trade union leaders and members to participate in lofty schemes that require unions to alter their basic bargaining tactics and to restructure themselves internally, for this participation calls for the presence on policy-making and/or planning boards of trade union representatives who are able, first, to protect their own interests and, second, to make a valuable contribution which has to be endorsed by the organizations they represent. Such a contribution is necessary if these national economic and/or political schemes are to work.

Trade unions have become accustomed to serving as whipping boys for those who seek to explain away the failure of a ruling government's attempts to meet its economic and political challenges. Unions have been held to be at least partly responsible for the failure of both broad and short-range economic and political reforms. They have been condemned for their alleged recalcitrance and labeled as villains by both friend and foe alike.

In a society which is generally ignorant of trade union goals, functions, and methods, a tendency exists for misinformed individuals to view unions as anachronistic in an age of allegedly "enlightened" management, higher wages, and improved standards of living. In their view, employee discontent should now be nonexistent, and any hostilities between labor and management (including strikes) should lessen or disappear. The failure of this to happen has created considerable public obfuscation. Many employers have likewise been of the opinion that employee contentment should increase correspondingly with higher wages and improved working conditions; and it is certainly true that both remuneration and working conditions have improved vastly during the past several decades, due to the presence of effective unions at the job site battling for higher wages and seeking to make "industrial jurisprudence" an efficacious protective process.

Those who find themselves unable to understand continued worker militancy in industrial society will be just as bewildered under postindustrialism. They will consider workers to be selfish and unreasonable, ignoring the fact that the real causes of worker unrest lie deeper than wages and working conditions. As we have already pointed out, conflict in an employment situation is deeply rooted in the natural and unending desire of human beings to be free from the arbitrary actions of those in superior positions.[1] This is what V.L. Allen was referring to when he stated:

> No matter how strikes are viewed and which strikes are considered, they have two common characteristics. All the participants are employees, and their action is primarily directed against employers through a withdrawal of labour. Their cause must then be sought in the relationship between employees and employers. There must be something in this relationship which creates a permanent, though not always overt hostility.[2]

It is the employer who organizes the structure of the productive process and thereby the content of an individual's work. An employee's job is controlled by this unilateral, seemingly external source both quantitatively and qualitatively. Workers are forced to accept the impersonality of the forces which control their working life—the portion of their total life which makes the rest possible. The *quid pro quo* is compensation in the form of money and working conditions. This was true of industrial society, and it is and will be true of postindustrial society. Everything does not have a price in labor-management relations, however; the need and desire for job equity and, in some cases, job autonomy cannot be bought off with some form of remuneration. This will become increasingly evident in postindustrial society, which requires higher technological levels and employees with the abilities to make this new technology operable.

The suspicion which workers feel toward management enhances their reluctance to play this "new" role which is open for them in postindustrial society. An increased incidence of strikes may be an indication of their hesitation to break with the past. Trade unions will continue to represent workers who are reacting to their environment, and the fact that this environment has changed will permit workers to reach a degree of societal influence which was unobtainable in industrial society. Using the economic power base which they have established vis-à-vis employers through collective bargaining, trade unions will be able to exercise a broader influence upon postindustrial society, but they will have to convince their membership of the advantages of doing so if they are to make effective use of this opportunity.

Failure to make the most of their societal power position will not necessarily cause trade unions to atrophy, for they still have their role to play as combatants on the job site. It would, however, represent a lost opportunity for labor to play a political role which was impossible before the evolution into postindustrial society.

The role of the government is also decisive in obtaining trade union participation and cooperation at the policy-making level. This is, of course, more likely to occur when a "friendly" administration is in power. The danger lies in the inability of a government to convince the trade union movement that it is in its own best interests to function realistically at a policy-making level—a role which labor has only experienced to any real extent during wartime. Some unions, of course, will never trust either a ruling government or employers enough to cooperate with them on any level, let alone a national one which is remote from the shop floor. But others will fail to do so because the government has not convinced them that they have a vital and necessary new role to play as the representatives of workers.

The initial feedback which unions receive from such participation must be both dramatic and visible to the rank and file if labor cooperation is to continue. It is all too easy for trade unions to fall back into the position of mere bargaining organizations, failing to realize their postindustrial political potential. For them to continue to function politically as lobbying organizations, because of a disbelief in the possibility of their acting effectively at a policy-making level in a restructured pluralistic democracy, indicates a failure on the part of government.[3]

This is why Mark van de Vall's vision of a trade union movement placing the interests of its memberhip second to some higher, societal calling is unlikely to be fulfilled. In postindustrial society, trade unions will continue to operate as organizations reacting to their environment—but the important thing to remember is that their environment will have changed. Trade unions will thus have to demonstrate a flexibility in methods in seeking what Victor Allen has previously termed their "primary aim." While continuing to do battle at the level of the job or occupation, unions will also be able—given an economic power base—to function on a societal plane dealing with a broader range of issues which directly or indirectly affect their membership.

A new activism will become apparent in postindustrial society. The vast changes in technology, the labor force, and the societal power structure will create an unprecedented degree of unrest among employees. The uneasy balance which governments have attempted to reach in industrial societies will develop into a malaise in postindustrial society, and economic instability will be substituted for the consensus of earlier times. Typically, employers will attempt to crush this activity, or they will try to buy workers off. Governments have been, and will be, more cognizant than employers of the need to deal with this activism, and those that are interested in staying in power will lead the way in the creation of mechanisms to channel this new militance in constructive ways. If they are to be successful, they must make real attempts to bring labor (and management) into policy-making positions which are demonstrative of actual, not imagined change. Facades must be avoided like the plague.

Basic restructuring is called for, remembering the persistence of differing interests in postindustrial society. A union policy which endorses the pursuance of the maximum economic rewards may force a government to seek such restructuring,[4] especially if unions continue to view high wages as a sign of progress, not as a crime in a new society in which a government has attempted to establish new regulations under which a new "web of rules" may be developed.[5]

If economic and political priorities are to be democratically established in a postindustrial society, a form of bargaining must be created involving societal interest groups whose activities can negate the goals being sought. The experience under postindustrialism will demonstrate that class conflicts for power will continue

> with the state now also the arena for these conflicts. Each group and class including organized labor seeks the freedom to express itself and to bargain for its views, interests, and priorities on all fronts, economic, political, and social. The continuing accommodation of their respective claims through mutual concessions and compromise is vital to national survival.[6]

Younger workers comprise the primary source of this new activism, but women, white-collar, professional, and technical employees are also in its forefront. Postindustrial society has created new sources of frustration and uneasiness among these workers, who are impatient with the rate of change in economic and social conditions. In the United States the first evidence of this is increases in the numbers (and perhaps the length) of strikes, and increasing rates of absenteeism and work force turnover within a firm. The trade unions representing these workers must reflect their members' expectations and aspirations if they are to retain the activists within their ranks and thus make use of this new source of militancy. The unrest which is just beginning to confront employers (and indeed trade unions and society also) may be resolved by a series of gains at the job site accompanied by larger, more significant changes in the basic structure of employment relations in postindustrial society.

In postindustrial society, the trade union will continue to serve as the sanctioned channel for the expression of workers' dissatisfaction with present conditions. It is the instrument which can be used directly by employees in their job-site confrontations with employers and in their dealings with the polity. If worker aspirations are to become something besides mere rhetoric, trade unions must be able to function effectively at two levels, and they owe it to their membership to be able to deal with employers in their role as employers and with employers (and other interest groups) at a higher, political level. It is at this second level that the sheer adversary role of labor on the job site must fade and give way to a more conciliatory and less doctrinaire approach. Here trade unions must be more "flexible in strategy and responsive to new proposals and experiments."[7] The attributes which correlate with job-site militancy must acquiesce to this second function. The independence which trade unions have been able to maintain between themselves and their societal allies serves only to add to their ability and power to function at this second level. The result is "that unions have been able to press their positions even more vigorously than before. The new determination extends to industrial relations as well as broad public issues, particularly as these relate to the domestic economy. *The attainment of the goal is primary; the method, secondary.*"[8]

Trade Unions and Economic Planning

It is in the area of national economic planning that trade unions will play their most distinctive, unique, and novel role in the postindustrial polity. The great impetus for national economic planning in Western Europe followed World War II, when a new relationship between trade unions and the polity in Western democracies began to emerge. By that time, unions had firmly established themselves as part of the economic and political scene, and new forms of stress were being placed upon organized labor.

These pressures, which marked the beginning of a new era in labor history, were more severe in Western Europe than in the United States because of the havoc wreaked by the war and the scope of the needed rebuilding process. The year 1945 saw the governments of Western Europe attempting to establish programs of economic recovery through indicative planning, involving the government and both labor and management. Incomes policies were created (or attempts were made to create them) as part of national programs setting economic priorities, and it was hoped that involving trade unions in these schemes at the policy-making level would give them a greater stake in the successful operation of the plans. Accordingly, ruling governments called upon trade unions to play a more "mature" role than had been the case in the prewar period.

The reactions of most trade union movements were positive, although it must be admitted that their participation was not always for purely altruistic reasons. As their surroundings had dramatically changed, unions realized that they would have to pursue different courses of behavior to achieve their primary aims.

> There is no difficulty about defining the aims of trade unions. It is acknowledged universally that their prime aim, and the one from which others flow, is to protect and improve the living standards of their members. Industrial societies are such a complexity of interdependent parts that action in pursuit of the prime aim has to be taken in diverse ways and at different levels. . . . A trade union which is alert to the interests of its members has to be perceptive and responsive not only to changes in the work situation but also to changes in its environment in general.[9]

Cooperation with the polity and with employers or employers' associations therefore replaced the sheer adversary position assumed by many unions in the past. This approach was encouraged by the various cooperative efforts which trade unions in the United States, Great Britain, and Canada had engaged in during World War II.

Nevertheless, trade unions were often suspicious that these planning attempts were nothing but a sham, making no real changes in the structure of the economy.[10] Given an apparent acceptance of capitalism, the trade unions could see no need or advantage to be gained from moderating their wage demands. In Great Britain, for example, the trade unions exhorted the Labour government to establish a planned socialist economy but were reluctant to continue their initial sacrifices when they saw no dramatic alteration in Britain's economic structure and no attempt to redistribute income or wealth. What they did envision was the destruction of the basis of their power in society—their economic bargaining with employers as a way to more directly benefit their membership. The *quid pro quo* which was mentioned as being an essential part of any changed relationship between the trade unions and the polity in postindustrial society has not been apparent to the unions in the industrial nations of Western Europe. In addition, trade unions hesitated to make the sacrifices asked of them and to carry out the internal changes required of them if economic planning was to work when a nonlabor government took power (as often happened in the 1950s).

The reasons for the failure of these planning attempts and structures are many. In some instances, they were never totally accepted by either labor or management. In spite of the fact that government has traditionally played a larger role in the economies of Western Europe than is the case in the United States,* many firms found these programs to be an interference as time progressed.

The features of the incomes policies contained in these plans were also met with trade union resistance, and unions felt that they were being singled out as a disruptive force in the economy when restrictions were placed upon their wage bargaining with employers. Certainly the attempts in the Netherlands to formally establish wage differentials serve as an example of this.[11]

Nonetheless, signs of change have been and are present in Western Europe. Those who mourn the failure to establish a planned *socialist* economic order might be mollified somewhat by the fact that the nature of capitalism in these indus-

---

*This goes beyond direct intervention in the economy. In these countries, where nationalization of industry is much more common and accepted than in the United States, its function as an employer causes government to play a larger economic role, often attempting to establish itself as a "model" employer.

trial nations has been subject to change. It has been claimed that the "success of the modern capitalist society in reversing the pressures making for high consumption at the expense of investment is one of its outstanding achievements."[12] This transference from consumption to investment is one of the goals of economic planning.

Andrew Shonfield would also have us believe that an equally dramatic characteristic of the "new capitalism" lies in its human aspect, that is, in the establishment of the mechanisms of the welfare state. He claims that the capitalist systems of Western Europe have been so dramatically altered that they bear little resemblance to those of the past; that environmental pressures have forced changes and reforms upon these capitalist systems for the betterment of the general citizenry; that the future continuation of capitalism as an economic system has been reinforced. This argument is comparable to the claim that the programs of Franklin D. Roosevelt's New Deal were the saviors of capitalism, not its destroyers.

In describing the approaches to national economic planning in industrial Western Europe in the 1950s and 1960s, Shonfield cites three factors which permeate these systems, and have caused them to take their present form: a steady rate of economic growth, an extremely rapid increase in production, and the wide diffusion of the benefits of the "new prosperity."[13] In discussing the new balance of power between the private sector and the government in modern capitalist societies, he uses as examples France, Great Britain, Italy, Austria, and Sweden. These are compared to countries with "market ideologies," such as the United States and Germany. But even in these latter two countries, the public interest is playing a larger role in the operation of private enterprise without the establishment of formal planning devices.

Many of the plans which Shonfield dealt with have not evolved as he predicted. Certainly he did not foresee the virtual collapse of economic planning in Great Britain. Nevertheless, the political implications of a more active role of government in these planned capitalist economies bears some signficance for postindustrial conditions. "The political institutions in current use in Western society were designed, for the most part, to cope with a set of circumstances that are remote from those"[14] which presently exist in industrial society, and they are certainly different from those which do and will exist in postindustrial society.

The relationship between the individual citizen and the state, and the presence of collective entities such as trade unions and other organized pressure groups, demand a revision of the role of postindustrial government. The vulnerability of the citizen as worker to the power of the enterprise and the state will undergo significant alterations. This is especially true of individuals who have a trade union to protect their interests in an organized society, but the benefits derived from collective organization around a job or occupation will also drift down to the unorganized workers.

A government facing the dilemma of balancing the control of democratic practices while accepting and permitting its citizenry's exercise of political liberties must develop safeguards if this balance is to be maintained. While officials must be allowed the opportunity to act effectively, they must be subject to controls; that is, devices must be established whereby elected or appointed governmental officials can be held accountable for their acts. If government is going to play the role called for in postindustrial society, it must develop the expertise required for such functioning. Additionally, the interplay among government, labor, management, and other vested interest groups has to be clearly defined and open to public review. While a pluralistic society abhors monoliths, there will be a tendency for the powerful pressure groups in postindustrial society to exercise their function without control from below.

It has already been pointed out that the increased militancy of the new unions will create and guarantee this control from below, but the same cannot be said for other pressure groups. Thus the creation of public controls over these groups is called for. This is especially important in the case of the government technocrat, whose expertise few elected officials can match. In order to control the governmental technocracy, expertise on the staffs of elected officials is therefore necessary, as is direct feedback from the citizenry.[15] While the presence of expertise on the part of the new parochial interest groups which will play a partnership type of role with government will provide checks on and perhaps restrict governmental actions, the government will have to be able to exercise corresponding checks over the activities of these organized interest groups. The danger of the corporate state is one which haunts postindustrial society.

National economic planning in postindustrial societies will attempt to establish priorities regarding the allocation of resources and income distribution. The process will bear some resemblance to the system of "pluralistic industrialism" predicted by the authors of *Industrialism and Industrial Man,* and will draw upon the experience of market-oriented economies in dealing with the problems of economic growth, inflation, and the establishment of economic stability.[16] It will be a complex procedure, indicative in nature, involving all parties that possess both a vested interest in the policies established and a type of veto power which can prevent them from being effectively carried out. The presence in society of new power groups will force the government to involve these new organizations in the planning process if democracy is to be maintained; that is, if government-directed imperative planning is to be avoided.

While trade unions have a vital interest in the establishment of national priorities, the portion of indicative planning systems of most direct concern to them is that dealing with incomes policies. A general feeling on the part of trade unions— one that will continue to exist in postindustrial society—is that improvements in a worker's standard of living can be accomplished either through technological improvements which increase the income level of the population in general while leaving the relative positions of income earners unchanged, or through a redistribution of income.[17] The dilemma facing the unions will be whether to seek this redistribution of income through collective bargaining or by using the route of governmentally sanctioned income policies. History indicates that they will choose the former.

Trade unions have traditionally demonstrated greater faith in their own ability to obtain wage increases, and thereby indirectly redistribute income, than in legislative schemes. While unions have fully endorsed efforts to legislatively establish and raise minimum levels of income for the general populace, this activity has been an auxiliary function to the unions' primary goal—protecting and pursuing the interests of the membership to whom they are responsible. This method— collective bargaining—is more visible to union members and also more readily understandable. While both new and old unionists in postindustrial society will be aware of the diffusive effects of the economic gains which they have won through collective action, this is not of primary concern to them. They did not join or form trade unions to have these organizations participate in some vague program of income redistribution. When they opt for collective action vis-à-vis their employer, their intention is to benefit themselves in a direct and immediate fashion.

An additional question must be raised regarding the ability of a government, acting either alone or in concert with trade unions, to implement an incomes policy successfully. The basic determinant of the income received by an individual covered by a collective agreement is the power of the organization representing his interests with his employer. There is a dangerous undemocratic tendency in allowing a higher authority to decide just what an individual is worth to society. Any attempt to tie wage or salary increases to increases in productivity also runs into difficulties, because it raises basic questions about the relative contributions to productivity made by the human element and by capital investments and technological improvements. Employees have a natural tendency to view attempts to tie monetary increments to productivity gains as more beneficial to management than to themselves; and they also fear that such increases in productivity will lead to decreases in the size of an enterprise's work force.[18] The problem becomes more complex in postindustrial society where the economy is service oriented. A tertiary or service-oriented economy is by definition labor intensive, and the nature of the service or tertiary sector makes productivity difficult if not impossible to measure accurately.

Added to the difficulty of establishing and running an incomes policy is the fear on the part of both American labor and management that control over wages must invariably lead to control over prices, and that this will lead to further unilateral control by government over the entire industrial relations system as it has developed in the United States. It is also feared that government will use wage policy as a wedge to extend its control over production, which contradicts the intermediary role that government will play in postindustrial society. While it is predicted that the societal power exerted by autonomous groups will prevent such governmental action, the fear of unilaterally imposed control by government is still present. Whether this is real or imaginary is less important than the fact that the fear exists, and its existence may make a working incomes policy impossible, or at least extremely difficult.

A survey of the attempts by the governments of Western European countries to establish an incomes policy indicates that they have not been very successful; they have been unable to combine full employment with price stability. Perhaps these plans were too ambitious, but this alone cannot explain their failure. No Western European government has been able to overcome the obstacles which have already been discussed. Moral suasion has not been effective, and the centralization called for on both the part of trade unions and employers has not taken place to any noticeable degree. In addition, these nations have understandably been unwilling to pay the price which might make such policies actually work—the imposition of unilateral legislative enforcement. The governments concerned are aware of the dangers that such compulsory policies may lead to—the dramatic alteration of parliamentary democracy.[19] The question which must be dealt with here is what this experience portends for postindustrial society.

The answer lies in the basic differences between industrial and postindustrial society. In the former, attempts at economic planning and the creation of incomes policies were viewed with suspicion by the trade unions, whose cooperation was essential and even vital to the success of these schemes. When cooperation did occur, it was too often merely a defensive reaction on the part of the trade union movement, which was (and still is) fearful that compulsory measures would take the place of voluntary cooperation. This defensiveness resulted in a token acceptance of such schemes and something less than wholehearted participation in them. There was a very obvious tendency to view the proposals for some sort of economic partnership as being nothing but a chimera. Richard Pryke's treatment in *Though Cowards Flinch* of the attempts at economic planning by Harold Wilson's Labour government in Great Britain provides just such an example.

The extensive nature of the power base which organized labor will be able to create in postindustrial society will force governments, be they friendly or unfriendly, to call for trade union participation in the setting and achievement of economic targets. No loss of freedom will accompany the successful working of economic planning because the economic power (and the political power derived from this economic base) of both labor and management will doom such plans to failure if their participation is not sought. The trade unions which will be most amenable to such participation are those that have firmly recognized and fulfilled their primary function. These are likely to be unions representing the "new" employees in the total labor force. The more aggressive position which these unions will assume at the bargaining table will be reflected in their willingness to reinforce the gains they have made through bargaining by participating in broader societal schemes.

While trade union participation in such adventures and co-operation with the polity in all probability will initially be due to a desire to protect their members' interests, the unions will eventually realize the full potential open to them. Based on the Western European experience, they will be able to play a creative role in shaping government policies which are directly related to the functioning of the economy and the relative economic position of the people they represent. But they will find themselves able to exert a degree of influence on more marginal issues which will be possible only under post-industrialism. Instead of merely attempting to influence government policy on a broad range of political issues, they (and other groups) will be consulted by government before these policies are established. Ever cognizant of the basis of their societal power, trade unions will be able to exert their influence and power in a more positive manner, thus allowing their members to influence what were formerly impersonal forces that controlled their off-the-job existence. While representative democracy will continue to exist politically for the individual citizen, the trade union member will have the added leverage of union representation on a variety of issues. The positions which trade unions will take will be determined not by their leadership, but by the process of representative democracy internal to the labor organization itself. Postindustrial society will have to allow the participation of unions at the policy-making level because of the increased presence of labor in the political arena. Instead of merely exercising veto power, trade unions and their confederations will reach an accommodation with the polity which will insure the continuation of pluralistic democracy. Postindustrial society will create powerful pressure groups, or enhance the power of already existing pressure groups, which will make totalitarianism an impossibility.

Trade Unions and Workers' Control

A method which originated with the socialist labor movements of the nineteenth century—and which still resides in the ideology of Catholic and other trade unions today—is the idea of co-management of enterprise. The philosophical drive for some sort of workers' control was reinforced by the well known papal encyclicals "Quadregisimo Anno" and "Rerum Novarum." While the right of private property was accepted, "substantial alteration in the rights and practice of ownership"[20] was sought. The movement for workers' control also can be traced back to the syndicalist movements which existed in both Mediterranean Europe and the United States. These divergent origins help to explain the various meanings of the idea for its present-day proponents.

Workers' control exists today in Western Europe in the form of workers' councils at the job-site level, mechanisms for joint consultation, and worker representation on the boards of directors which govern an enterprise. Workers' councils exist both in Western and Eastern Europe. In Germany, the councils act in the absence of local unions as they are known in the United States. They have both advisory power and, in some areas, an authority equal to that of the employer. In Yugoslavia, they are part of a national scheme which provides for the governance of industry with the consent of the workers on the shop floor. Western European trade unions tend to view them in one of two ways: either as substitutes for actual trade unionism or as devices designed to be supportive of unionism itself. Councils can also be classified by distinguishing between those that act as administrative representatives on the job site and those that actually engage in some type of collective bargaining with management.[21]

Joint consultation exists in Great Britain at the plant level. This process involves the voluntary establishment of joint committees in which management deals with representatives of the workers (who may also be union stewards). Consultations are generally on matters of production, but may cover a broader range of issues which are of concern to management.

The form of workers' control of greatest relevance to the American experience is that which mandates the presence of representatives directly chosen by the workers on the board of directors of a firm. The theory behind such schemes is to involve the individual worker at the highest levels of the decision-making process affecting his daily existence. This type of workers' control or participation in management has attracted a great deal of interest and experimentation in democratic economies,[22] especially since the time of the economic recovery programs initiated in Western Europe at the end of World

War II. While the experiment in co-determination in the German coal and steel industries has received the greatest amount of attention, current economic developments have renewed interest in forms of worker participation in management decision making.

The German experiment with this form of workers' control can be traced back to ideas promulgated around the middle of the nineteenth century. Its more immediate history dates from about 1950, when disillusionment with the outcome of the nationalization of industry became evident. In addition to establishing relative parity of representation on the supervisory board (the equivalent of the part-time positions of American members of a firm's board of directors), the law providing for co-determination in German coal and steel mandates the appointment of a "labor director" to the full-time managing board of a firm in these two industries. Outside of the German coal and steel industries, the law mandates that one-third of the total members of the board of directors of a joint stock company must be directly elected by the workers employed by a firm. While studies made of the German experiment with co-determination have indicated a tendency to "humanize" the relationship between labor and management, its effects have proved difficult to measure. Although co-determination has served as the catalyst for comparable movements in other countries, the device is often viewed with suspicion by trade unionists who consider it a gimmick to increase productivity at the expense of increased wages.[23]

While workers' councils at the job site are viewed as devices to prevent the presence of an actual trade union and true bilateralism at the level of production of a product or the performance of a service, the problem with attempts to mandate worker representation at the highest levels of the corporate hierarchy is that while they may have changed the decision-making structure at this level, they have not made themselves felt at the level of the job site.

> In terms of broader objectives, participation, even at best, has had limited success. It has involved top leadership far more than the rank and file, and it has almost ignored lower and middle levels of management. It has not brought power and influence to the ordinary worker; nor has it unleashed workers' creativity or even actively involved the leadership in making production decisions. The division of labor between decision-makers and those who carry out decisions has not been abolished.[24]

The relevance of these experiments for postindustrial society leads directly to the authority structure inherent to all employment relationships. While the labor director in German coal and steel may humanize industrial relations, he is still part of the managerial hierarchy; he is an order giver. If he continues to behave as a representative of the order takers, he cannot fulfill the duties delegated to him. The greater likelihood is that he will "adapt" to his new role and become part of management.[25]

As is the case in industrial society, in postindustrial society these types of attempts at workers' participation assume a continuity or convergence of interest between management and labor. A cooperative attempt at problem solving is so overemphasized that it becomes a chimera which workers will quickly see through. While it is true that workers and their unions do have a vested interest in the continued successful operation of their employer whether it be in the private or the public sector, the notion of workers' participation or co-management flies in the face of the fact that there has to be an authority structure in any employing enterprise; that conflict, or the potential for conflict, is a fact of life whenever there are order givers and order takers.

Even if these attempts at worker or union participation at the higher levels of management are well intentioned, they have little, if any, effect on the ever-present authority structure. Their failure can best be understood when one views trade unions as organizations whose primary function is to protect and promote the job-related interests of their membership. Whether an individual be an unskilled worker or a professional, the immediate effect of union activity which is of concern to the union member is that which deals with the individual as an employee; that is, a person who is subjected to an authority structure.[26]

When workers' control assumes the form of substitute unionism, the dangers both internal and external to the employment siutation of unilateral decision making appear, and the benefits of bilateralism disappear. On the other hand, when workers' control is aimed at the higher levels of an employing enterprise, it is working in the wrong direction. The basic conflict in postindustrial society as regards programs for workers' control is between the realities of an employment situation and social visionaries.

7

Conclusion and
Some Unanswered Questions

The structure, role, and function of trade unions in postindustrial society has to be viewed within the larger context of the concept of the social order. There are two polarized theories of social order which are most vividly seen in the conflicting works of two sociologists: Talcott Parsons and Ralf Dahrendorf. The first might be termed the integration theory of society. It views "social structure in terms of a functionally integrated system held in equilibrium by certain patterned and recurrent processes,"[1] and claims that social order results from a general consensus. The second is a coercion theory of society, presenting a conception of "social structure as a form of organization held together by force and constraint and reaching continuously beyond itself in the sense of producing within itself the forces that maintain it in an unending process of change."[2] Clearly the theory of trade unions in postindustrial society developed in this book fits into the second, conflict-oriented theory of social structure.

Assuming the consistent presence of conflict in postindustrial society, two approaches may be taken to deal with it. The first is to assume a position of intolerance of internal dissent— to establish a rigid social structure from which deviations are not permitted. The social structure created by Communist nations is illustrative of this technique. Its ineffectiveness can be demonstrated by the inability of these totalitarian nations to totally crush deviations from the established societal norms, and in the modifications of these systems by such deviationist countries as Yugoslavia.

The second approach recognizes the inevitability of internal dissent and conflict, and provides flexibility within the system to deal with it. In so doing, it allows dissenting groups and voices to be heard, develops mechanisms to channel this dissent into constructive forms, and thus integrates the dissenters into the existing social order.[3] This assimilation process permits real, not imagined, adaptations to take place in society. Under this approach, the recognition of conflict as a natural phenomenon is the major device by which the social order is held together. This resembles the "unending process of change" recognized by the coercion theory of society, and it is the essence of a realistic approach to the presence of organized labor and the dramatic changes which are forced upon postindustrial society.

Within the context of a conflict-oriented society, there are definite advantages for both trade unions and employers—and indirectly for the ruling government—in dealing with each other as organized entities. This is of greater concern to the postindustrial employer than the postindustrial trade union. By definition, employers have a formal organization structure including positions of authority and responsibility and a set of enterprise-wide goals governing a system of smaller group goals. Just as it "is difficult for a modern army to deal with the tactics of guerrilla bands,"[4] it is difficult for such an organization to deal with the tactics of an unorganized group of workers. While an employer may not be overjoyed with the prospect of having his authority challenged by his employees, the use of collective bargaining—under ground rules established by legislation—to channel employee protest and demands provides a structure and predictability which would otherwise be lacking. While both labor and management are free to choose their own course of action within the framework set up by government, a degree of order is provided for the process.

Additionally, a degree of cohesiveness on the part of both parties facilitates the resolution of conflict through collective bargaining. Once an agreement is reached, an employer is assured that it will be adhered to because the union's structure and extent of organization makes it possible for it to enforce the contract successfully. A trade union which is certain of its continued organizational existence provides a more realistic opponent for an employer to face than one which is uncertain of its future. Also, a well-organized adversary is more likely to fight with accepted weapons, those that have been sanctioned by society.[5]

This degree of institutionalization of conflict bothers some people who fear that the individual will be ignored by his union and thus face a form of alienation and frustration emanating from both his work environment and the organization which is supposed to represent his interests. However, the activist and militant nature of the new postindustrial worker makes it unlikely that a union will be unresponsive to its members' perceived needs and demands.

A successful and viable postindustrial trade union will recognize that its primary function is to represent the concerns of its membership as they pertain to the employment environment. It cannot be expressed strongly enough that the secret of the postindustrial trade union is its ability to develop the community of interest which emanates from job-related issues and to translate this into other areas—always, though, areas which support at least in part the primary trade union purpose as recognized by the membership and their elected leaders. Should a union or its leadership forget this important lesson, either the union will self-destruct or the leadership will be replaced. The greater militancy and impatience of the postindustrial worker/trade-union member makes this inevitable. Internal union democracy will be a much more vigorous process than it has been in the past.

The alleged alienation of the postindustrial worker is of concern to his union, and it will be dealt with by that union at the two levels which have been discussed before: the job site and the larger societal level. There are some jobs into which it is impossible to build any sort of self-actualization for the worker. For individuals in these positions, the establishment of on-the-job bilaterally determined and conducted systems of jurisprudence, off-the-job improvements in their standard of living, and the increased societal influence they are able to exercise through their union will have to suffice. But the type of worker who will assume a position of predominance in postindustrial society will be able to channel his new militancy into creative forms which will make his work itself a meaningful process as far as possible.

As Irving Kristol points out,

> The fact that young workers are more insistently demanding a middle-class life style will hardly suggest, to the disinterested observer, that they are an "alienated" class. To reach such a conclusion, you have to be an "alienated" sociologist. Of these, alas, we seem to have an abundant supply.[6]

In a 1973 address to the University Labor Education Association, William W. Winpisinger, then general vice president and currently president of the International Association of Machinists and Aerospace Workers, dealt with the issues of worker alienation and job enrichment and refuted the idea that workers feel dehumanized or alienated. He pointed out, first, that less than 2 percent of the American labor force is engaged in assembly line operations which are generally considered the epitome of the alienated job, and contended that what an intellectual views as satisfying work is not necessarily what the majority of the labor force seeks from employment. He stated that these workers are not in search of self-fulfillment; they work to earn a paycheck. The ability to confront superiors on a daily basis through the grievance machinery established by collective bargaining fills the void for the worker which the work itself does not fill. He views drives for job enrichment as devices created to increase not worker contentment but worker efficiency. It is a facade by which greater productivity is achieved at the expense of a reduced work force; the penalty coincident with job enrichment (and increased productivity) is job displacement. The workers themselves will receive no financial benefits from such proposals because that is not their purpose.

For employees whose jobs require a great deal of education and training, the possibility of self-fulfillment from employment may not come automatically; it may have to be forced from an employer at the bargaining table. These individuals are not afraid of working themselves out of a job. They illustrate the agressive/offensive, innovative, and creative side of what has been referred to as the nonmanualist psychology, and their unions will reflect this attitude. For those "new" workers employed in positions from which some comparable sense of job autonomy or self-fulfillment is not possible, unions will make demands similar to those of the unions of industrial society whose members view work as a means to an end.

For this latter group of workers, the broader social and political programs which their unions will embark on will help to replace the meaning they do not find in their work. While unions of professional and technical employees are likely to be more receptive to the new societal role which trade unions will play in postindustrial society, the more "traditional" trade unions will also take advantage of these new opportunities that are available to them.

Further changes toward broader political and social action involving the mass of members appear quite unavoidable as the present measures prove inadequate to deal with our economic reverses. Established patterns of activities within the movement which accent collective bargaining and bread-and-butter unionism will not deter the organization from moving into the wider arena. . . . The trade-union's test of tactics is performance not theory.[7]

Trade unions have traditionally been more flexible in adjusting and changing their tactics than have the more dogmatic and doctrinaire political parties, and unions have used their political programs in limited, though effective, ways. In the American context, the independence which trade unions have maintained from any organic ties with a political party is ideal for political trade union activities in a postindustrial setting. The fact that the tactics of the trade union movement have never been fixed adds to the likelihood that these organizations will respond innovatively to the new challenges facing them.

These responses will initially be cautious. Organized labor will not easily be pressed into changing (or as some would have us believe, deserting) the patterns of behavior established during an evolutionary process which began before the turn of the nineteenth century. The primary focus on job-related matters which trade unions must and will demonstrate prevents them from meeting any rendezvous with destiny. The law of gradualism is inherent in the *raison d'être* of these organized collectivities. By focusing on the real and immediate problems which their members face, trade unions will come up with programs that are dramatic and perhaps even radical, not in terms of any abstract theory, but in the context of concrete reality. Workers are not as a group short-sighted as regards actual, progressive change.

In fact all such discussions overlook the reality that basic progressive change does not spring from the reading of obscure and abstract manifestos. Rather it comes from the real and immediate needs of ordinary people. A majority of the participants in the American Revolution never heard of John Locke. The mobs that stormed the Bastille in France in 1789 did not know that a writer named Voltaire even existed. What "common" people know are their problems and that palliatives won't solve them.[8]

It has been claimed that the basic cause of breakdowns in capitalist economies is "the anarchic or planless character of capitalistic production."[9] This will not be the case in postindustrial society. The collective organization of nonmanual employees will create a trade union movement whose activities in the pursuit of its primary function will result in the agreements reached at the bargaining table having a far greater effect on the national economy than was true in the past. Some form of rational planning will eventually take place to prevent the tendency toward economic anarchy. This is why, in our model of postindustrial unionism, we have stressed the importance of their functioning on two levels. Fulfilling its primary function will enable organized labor to play an effective role on the secondary, societal level. Government may encourage this new role of trade unions or view it with reluctance, but labor's participation and cooperation is necessary if the benefits made possible by the evolution into postindustrialism are to be realities.

A welfare state, a younger and more highly educated labor force, a relative degree of affluence, and the evolution into a tertiary, service-oriented economy will not decrease the need for collective organization and action among employees. While there will be a similarity between some white-collar unions and their blue-collar predecessors, a new type of trade unionism will emerge along with the more highly educated and trained professional and technical employee. Even though this new type of organization will be more aggressive and less scarcity conscious than unions of employees with less degrees of training, it will be the result of the same universal phenomenon—the presence of an authority structure in all employing enterprises. This authority structure will be met with less blind acceptance and more hostility by the "new" worker. The prophets of doom who claim that organized labor has reached the pinnacle of its strength and extent of organization will prove to be as mistaken as those who choose to ignore employees' natural tendency to form collective organizations to achieve job-related goals which they cannot obtain as individuals.

It is recognized that the completion of this book leaves many questions unanswered. These provide possibilities for discussion and research, and will, I hope, be dealt with by others who recognize that the problems of postindustrialism pose a critical test for organized labor, threatening the very existence of trade unions as viable societal organizations. Although some may feel that the predictions made in this book have gone farther than the available data would allow, others may feel cheated in that it has not gone far enough or been definitive enough. I believe that this work has gone as far as possible in light of the factors mentioned in the preface.

Some of the questions left unresolved by this book deal with the role of women in the new labor movement, if indeed there is to be a new labor movement. The increased labor force participation rates of women may or may not be reflected by their presence in positions of influence within organized labor. Certainly, the evidence at the present time allows only for speculation here. The same holds for members of minority groups. We may hope that unions will prove wise enough to deal with this problem in a positive and decisive fashion and integrate the younger, more highly educated worker into positions of power regardless of race or sex. While the dual role of trade unions at the work site and on a societal plane has been suggested by others, especially Kassalow, the question remains whether organized labor will be able to perform this dual function, or whether the attempt will create a schizoid personality which will tear apart the very fiber that holds unions together. In fact, the effectiveness of trade unions in what is here termed the tertiary sector is called into question in light of the offensive, and in some cases counteroffensive, that employers utilize. The pervasiveness of the authority structure may not prove to be enough to break the reluctance of workers in the tertiary sector to take collective action vis-à-vis their employers. Certainly the challenge of the multi-industry, multinational corporation serves to reinforce this doubt.

It should be hoped that organized labor will prove itself able to meet the challenges of postindustrialism. Whether workers and their organizations do so in the manner predicted in this book will be seen over the next ten to twenty years.

Notes

Chapter 1

1. Gompers, *Seventy Years of Life and Labour*, pp. 286–87.
2. Rayback, *A History of American Labor*, p. 187.
3. Drucker, *The New Society*, p. 27.
4. Fite and Reese, *An Economic History of the United States*, p. 542.
5. Bunke, *American Economic History*, pp. 129–31.
6. Ibid., p. 129.
7. Bernstein, *The Lean Years*, p. 145.
8. See Cochran and Miller, *The Age of Enterprise*.
9. Fite and Reese, p. 544. "In 1920, A.T. & T. had only 139,448 stockholders compared to 469,801 in 1929; the number in United States Steel jumped from 95,776 to 182,000 during the same period."
10. Ibid., pp. 592–93.
11. Ibid., p. 593.
12. For a brief discussion of the Wagner Act see Bernstein, *The Turbulent Years*, pp. 318–51.
13. Heilbroner, "Economic Problems of a 'Postindustrial' Society," p. 164.
14. Fuchs, *The Service Economy*, p. 3.
15. Dahrendorf, *Class and Class Conflict in Industrial Society*, pp. 241–79.
16. Bell, "Labor in the Post-Industrial Society," pp. 163–89.
17. Campbell, *The Soviet-Type Economies*.
18. Kerr, Dunlop, Harbison, and Myers, *Industrialism and Industrial Man*, pp. 232–34.
19. Shonfield, *Modern Capitalism*, p. 335. Also see Chapter 13.
20. For a discussion of the experience in Western Europe and a comparison with the United States, see Klein, *The Management of Market-Oriented Economies*, Chapter 6, "Labor Organizations in Market-Oriented Economies."
21. Munson, *Indian Trade Unions*, p. 3.
22. Virgil B. Day quoted in Simkin, *Mediation and the Dynamics of Collective Bargaining*, p. 15.
23. Kassalow, *Trade Unions and Industrial Relations*, pp. 278–86.
24. Coser, *The Functions of Social Conflict*, pp. 105–7, 121–33.
25. Ibid., p. 126.
26. Gilmour and Lamb, *Political Alienation in Contemporary America*.
27. Bureau of Labor Statistics, *The U.S. Economy in 1980*, p. 19.
28. Gamson, *The Strategy of Social Protest*, pp. 130–43. The reader is also referred to the comprehensive volume by Smelser, *Theory of Collective Behavior*.

Chapter 2

1. All page numbers cited in parentheses in the text in this section refer to works of Norman Ware, abbreviated as follows: IW—*The Industrial Worker 1840–1860*; LM—*The Labor Movement in the United States 1860–1895*; LMIS—*Labor in Modern Industrial Society*.

2. Unless otherwise indicated, all page numbers cited in parentheses in the text in this section refer to Perlman, *Theory of the Labor Movement*.

3. John R. Commons and Associates, *History of Labour in the United States*, vol. II, part VI; Selig Perlman, "Upheaval and Reorganisation (Since 1876)," pp. 195–587.

4. Perlman, *A History of Trade Unionism in the United States*, pp. 285–94.

5. All page numbers cited in parentheses in the text in this section refer to Ely, *The Labor Movement in America*.

6. Commons, *Institutional Economics: Its Place in Political Economy*, vol. 2, pp. 677–84.

7. Commons and Associates, *History of Labour in the United States*, vol. 1, pp. 3–4.

8. Ibid., pp. 5–6, 9–10.

9. Commons, *Institutional Economics*, p. 767.

10. Commons, "American Shoemakers, 1648–1895: A Sketch of Industrial Evolution."

11. *Institutional Economics*, p. 767.

12. *Institutional Economics*, pp. 767–68; *Labor and Administration*, pp. 226–31. Also see Elias Lieberman, *Unions Before the Bar*.

13. *Institutional Economics*, pp. 768–73.

14. Commons, *Labor and Administration*, pp. 241–54.

15. Ibid., pp. 255–58.

16. Commons, *Legal Foundations of Capitalism*, pp. 134–42.

17. All page numbers cited in parentheses in the text in this section refer to works by Tannenbaum, abbreviated as follows: *LM—The Labor Movement: Its Conservative Functions and Consequences; PL—A Philosophy of Labor*.

18. All page numbers cited in parentheses in the text of this section refer to Hoxie, *Trade Unionism in the United States*.

19. All page numbers cited in parentheses in the text in this section refer to works by the Webbs, abbreviated as follows: *HTU—The History of Trade Unionism; ID—Industrial Democracy*.

20. Page numbers in parentheses in the text in this section refer to the following works: *CM*—Marx and Engels, *The Communist Manifesto; C—* Marx, *Capital; EPM*—Marx, *The Economic and Philosophic Manuscripts of 1844; WD*—Lenin, *What Is to Be Done?*

Chapter 3

1. All page numbers cited in parentheses in the text in this section refer to Lester, *As Unions Mature*.

2. Michels, *Political Parties*, pp. 349–56.

3. All page numbers cited in parentheses in the text in this section refer to van de Vall, *Labor Organizations*.

4. All page numbers cited in parentheses in the text in this section refer to Kerr et al., *Industrialism and Industrial Man*.

5. All page numbers cited in parentheses in the text in this section refer to Westley and Westley, *The Emerging Worker*.

6. All page numbers cited in parentheses in the text in this section refer to works by Goldthorpe et al., abbreviated as follows: *IAB—The Affluent Worker: Industrial Attitudes and Behaviour; PAB—The Affluent Worker: Political Attitudes and Behaviour; CS—The Affluent Worker in the Class Structure*.

7. All page numbers cited in parentheses in the text in this section refer to Munson, *Indian Trade Unions*.

8. All page numbers cited in parentheses in the text in this section refer to Gorz, *Strategy for Labor*.

9. All page numbers cited in parentheses in the text in this section refer to Montagna, *Occupations and Society.*

10. All page numbers cited in parentheses in the text in this section refer to Bell, *The Coming of Post-Industrial Society.*

11. For another view of unions in postindustrial society, see Touraine, *The Post-Industrial Society.*

Chapter 4

1. Dahrendorf, *Class and Class Conflict in Industrial Society,* p. 244.
2. Ibid., p. 259.
3. Ibid., pp. 257–79.
4. Kassalow, *Trade Unions and Industrial Relations: An International Comparison,* p. 41.
5. All page numbers cited in parentheses in the text in this section refer to Bureau of Labor Statistics, *The U.S. Economy in 1980.*
6. All page numbers cited in parentheses in the text in this section refer to Bureau of Labor Statistics, *The U.S. Economy in 1980.*
7. See Dahrendorf, especially Part Two; "Toward a Sociological Theory of Conflict in Industrial Society," pp. 157–318.
8. Kassalow, pp. 278–86.

Chapter 5

1. See Galbraith, *The New Industrial State.*
2. Ibid., pp. 3 and 274–76. See also Miernyk, *Trade Unions in the Age of Affluence,* p. 32.
3. Galbraith, p. 277.
4. *Alienation and Freedom: The Factory Worker and His Industry.*
5. Ibid., p. 157.
6. Ibid., pp. 124–65.
7. Dahrendorf, *Class and Class Conflict,* p. 254.
8. Ibid., pp. 548–57.

Chapter 6

1. Topham, "New Types of Bargaining," pp. 132–59.
2. Allen, *Militant Trade Unionism,* p. 112.
3. Schmidman, *British Unions and Economic Planning,* pp. 85–94.
4. Allen, *Militant Trade Unionism,* p. 158.
5. Jones, "Unions Today and Tomorrow," p. 124.
6. Barkin, "The Third Postwar Decade (1965–75): Progress, Activism, and Tension," in Barkin (ed.), *Worker Militancy and Its Consequences,* p. 37.
7. Barkin, "Summary and Conclusion: Redesigning Collective Bargaining and Capitalism," in Barkin (ed.), *Worker Militancy and Its Consequences,* p. 403.
8. Ibid., p. 404; emphasis added.
9. Allen, "The Paradox of Militance," p. 241.
10. See Schmidman, pp. 49–84.
11. See Edelman and Fleming, *The Politics of Wage-Price Decisions,* pp. 220–78.
12. Shonfield, *Modern Capitalism,* p. 6.
13. Ibid., p. 61
14. Ibid., p. 385.
15. Ibid., pp. 385–427.
16. Again see Klein, *The Management of Market-Oriented Economies: A Comparative Perspective.*

17. Allen, *Militant Trade Unionism*, pp. 150–51.
18. For a discussion of the experience in other countries see Galenson (ed.), *Incomes Policy: What Can We Learn From Europe?*
19. For another treatment of these policies and a discussion of future prospects see Ulman and Flanagan, *Wage Restraint: A Study of Incomes Policies in Western Europe.*
20. Kassalow, p. 174.
21. Sturmthal, *Workers Councils.*
22. The February 1970 issue of *Industrial Relations* was primarily devoted to a symposium on workers' participation in management.
23. Kassalow, pp. 180–87. Also see Sturmthal, *Comparative Labor Movements: Ideological Roots and Institutional Development*, pp. 65–75 and 87–100.
24. Strauss and Rosenstein, "Workers Participation: A Critical View," pp. 212–13.
25. Dahrendorf, pp. 263–64.
26. See Bendix, *Work and Authority in Industry*, pp. 1–21.

Chapter 7

1. Dahrendorf, *Class and Class Conflict*, p. 159.
2. Ibid.
3. Coser, *The Functions of Social Conflict*, pp. 95–97.
4. Ibid., p. 129.
5. Ibid., pp. 129–33.
6. Kristol, "Is the American Worker 'Alienated'?," p. 12. See this article for a brief discussion of worker alienation as the American economy becomes postindustrial.
7. Barkin, *Trade-Unions in an Age of Pluralism and Structural Change*, p. 820.
8. Levison, *The Working-Class Majority*, p. 282.
9. Heilbroner, *The Limits of American Capitalism*, p. 88.

Works Cited

Allen, V.L. *Militant Trade Unionism.* London: Merlin Press, 1966.

Allen, Victor. "The Paradox of Militance." In Robin Blackburn and Alexander Cockburn, *The Incompatibles: Trade Union Militancy and the Consensus.* Middlesex, England: Penguin Books, 1967, pp. 241–62.

Barkin, Solomon. *Trade-Unions in an Age of Pluralism and Structural Change.* Reprint Series, Number 33, Labor Relations and Research Center, University of Massachusetts, n.d.

———, ed. *Worker Militancy and Its Consequences, 1965–75.* New York: Praeger, 1975.

Bell, Daniel. *The Coming of Post-Industrial Society.* New York: Basic Books, 1973.

———. "Labor in the Post-Industrial Society." *Dissent* 19 (Winter 1972): 163–89.

Bendix, Reinhard. *Work and Authority in Industry.* New York: Harper Torchbooks, 1963.

Bernstein, Irving. "The Growth of American Unions." *The American Economic Review* 44, 3 (June 1954): 301–18.

———. *The Lean Years.* Baltimore: Penguin Books, 1966.

———. *Turbulent Years.* Boston: Houghton Mifflin, 1969.

Blauner, Robert. *Alienation and Freedom: The Factory Worker and His Industry.* Chicago: University of Chicago Press, 1964.

Bunke, Harvey C. *American Economic History.* New York: Random House, 1969.

Bureau of Labor Statistics. *The U.S. Economy in 1980.* BLS Bulletin 1673. Washington, D.C.: U.S. Department of Labor, 1970.

Campbell, Robert W. *The Soviet-Type Economies,* Boston: Houghton Mifflin, 1974.

Cochran, Thomas C., and Miller, William. *The Age of Enterprise.* New York: Macmillan, 1942.

Commons, John R. "American Shoemakers, 1648–1895: A Sketch of Industrial Evolution." *Quarterly Journal of Economics* 24 (November 1909): 39–81.

———. *Institutional Economics: Its Place in Political Economy.* 2 vols. Madison: University of Wisconsin Press, 1961; originally published by Macmillan, 1934.

———. *Labor and Administration.* New York: Augustus M. Kelley, 1964; originally published by Macmillan, 1913.

———. *Legal Foundations of Capitalism.* Madison: University of Wisconsin Press, 1959; originally published by Macmillan, 1924.

———— and Associates. *History of Labour in the United States.* 4 vols. New York: Augustus M. Kelley, 1966; original editions 1918 and 1935.

Coser, Lewis. *The Functions of Social Conflict.* New York: Free Press, 1956.

Dahrendorf, Ralf. *Class and Class Conflict in Industrial Society.* Stanford: Stanford University Press, 1959.

Donahue, Thomas R. In *John Herling's Labor Letter* 24, no. 21 (June 1, 1974): 3–4.

Drucker, Peter F. *The New Society.* New York: Harper and Row, 1960.

Edelman, Murray, and Fleming, R.W. *The Politics of Wage-Price Decisions.* Urbana: University of Illinois Press, 1965.

Ely, Richard T. *The Labor Movement in America.* New York: Arno Press, 1969; originally published by Thomas Y. Crowell, 1886.

Fite, Gilbert C., and Reese, Jim E. *An Economic History of the United States.* Boston: Houghton Mifflin, 1965.

Galbraith, John Kenneth. *The New Industrial State.* Boston: Houghton Mifflin, 1967.

Galenson, Walter, ed. *Incomes Policy: What Can We Learn From Europe?* Ithaca: New York State School of Industrial and Labor Relations, 1973.

Gamson, William A. *The Strategy of Social Protest.* Homewood, Ill.: Dorsey Press, 1975.

Gilmour, Robert S., and Lamb, Robert B. *Political Alienation in Contemporary America.* New York: St. Martin's Press, 1975.

Goldthorpe, John H.; Lockwood, David; Bechhofer, Frank; and Platt, Jennifer. *The Affluent Worker: Industrial Attitudes and Behaviour.* London: Cambridge University Press, 1968.

————. *The Affluent Worker: Political Attitudes and Behaviour.* London: Cambridge University Press, 1968.

————. *The Affluent Worker in the Class Structure.* London: Cambridge University Press, 1969.

Gompers, Samuel. *Seventy Years of Life and Labor.* New York: Augustus M. Kelley, 1967; first edition, E.P. Dutton, 1925.

Gorz, Andre. *Strategy for Labor.* Boston: Beacon Press, 1967; originally published in France as *Stratégie Ouvrière et Neocapitalisme,* Paris: Editions du Seuil, 1964.

Heilbroner, Robert L. *The Limits of American Capitalism.* New York: Harper and Row, 1965.

————. "Economic Problems of a 'Postindustrial' Society." *Dissent* 20 (Spring 1973): 163–76.

Hoxie, Robert F. *Trade Unionism in the United States.* New York: Russell & Russell, 1966; reprint of the second revised edition of 1923.

Jones, Jack. "Unions Today and Tomorrow." In *The Incompatibles: Trade Union Militancy and the Consensus,* ed. Robin Blackburn and Alexander Cockburn. Middlesex, England: Penguin Books, 1967, pp. 121–32.

Kassalow, Everett M. *Trade Unions and Industrial Relations: An International Comparison.* New York: Random House, 1969.

Kerr, Clark; Dunlop, John T.; Harbison, Frederick; and Myers, Charles A. *Industrialism and Industrial Man.* New York: Oxford University Press, 1964.

Klein, Philip A. *The Management of Market-Oriented Economies.* Belmont, Calif.: Wadsworth, 1973.

Kristol, Irving. "Is the American Worker Alienated?" *The Wall Street Journal,* January 18, 1973, p. 12.

Lenin, V.I. *What is to be Done?* New York: International Publishers, 1943; originally published 1902.

Lester, Richard. *As Unions Mature.* Princeton, N.J.: Princeton University Press, 1958.

Levison, Andrew. *The Working-Class Majority.* New York: Coward, McCann and Geoghegan, 1974.

Lieberman, Elias. *Unions Before the Bar.* New York: Oxford Book Company, 1960.

Marx, Karl. *Capital.* New York: The Modern Library; copyright 1906 by Charles H. Kerr and Company.

——. *The Economic and Philosophic Manuscripts of 1844,* New York, International Publishers, 1964.

——, and Engels, Friedrich. *The Communist Manifesto.* New York: Appleton-Century-Crofts, 1955; original edition 1848.

Michels, Robert. *Political Parties.* New York: Collier Books, 1962; originally published 1915.

Miernyk, William H. *Trade Unions in the Age of Affluence.* New York: Random House, 1962.

Montagna, Paul D. *Occupations and Society: Toward a Sociology of the Labor Market.* New York: John Wiley and Sons, 1977.

Munson, Fred C. *Indian Trade Unions.* Ann Arbor: Institute of International Commerce and Bureau of Industrial Relations, University of Michigan, 1970.

Perlman, Selig. *A Theory of the Labor Movement.* New York: Augustus M. Kelley, 1949; original edition 1928.

——. *A History of Trade Unionism in the United States.* New York: Augustus M. Kelley, 1950; originally published 1922.

Pryke, Richard. *Though Cowards Flinch.* London: Macgibbon and Kee, 1967.

Rayback, Joseph G. *A History of American Labor.* New York: Free Press, 1966.

Schmidman, John. *British Unions and Economic Planning.* University Park: Pennsylvania State University Press, 1969.

Shonfield, Andrew. *Modern Capitalism.* New York: Oxford University Press, 1970.

Simkin, William E. *Mediation and the Dynamics of Collective Bargaining.* Washington, D.C.: Bureau of National Affairs, 1970.

Smelser, Neil J. *Theory of Collective Behavior.* New York: Free Press, 1962.

Strauss, George, and Rosenstein, Eliezer. "Workers Participation: A Critical View." *Industrial Relations* 9, no. 2 (February 1970): 197–214.

Sturmthal, Adolph. *Workers Councils.* Cambridge, Mass.: Harvard University Press, 1964.

————. *Comparative Labor Movements: Ideological Roots and Institutional Development*. Belmont, Calif.: Wadsworth, 1972.

Tannenbaum, Frank. *A Philosophy of Labor*. New York: Alfred A. Knopf, 1951.

————. *The Labor Movement: Its Conservative Functions and Consequences*. New York: Arno Press, 1969; originally published by G.P. Putnam's Sons, 1921.

Topham, Tony. "New Types of Bargaining." In *The Incompatibles: Trade Unions Militancy and the Consensus*, ed. Robin Blackburn and Alexander Cockburn. Middlesex, England: Penguin Books, 1967, pp. 133–59.

Touraine, Alain. *The Post-Industrial Society: Tomorrow's Social History: Classes, Conflicts and Culture in the Programmed Society*. New York: Random House, 1971; originally published in France as *La Societe post industrielle*, Paris: Editions Denoel S.A.R.L., 1969.

Ulman, Lloyd, and Flanagan, Robert J. *Wage Restraint: A Study of Incomes Policies in Western Europe*. Berkeley: University of California Press, 1971.

van de Vall, Mark. *Labor Organizations*. London: Cambridge University Press, 1970.

Ware, Norman J. *The Industrial Worker 1840–1860*. Chicago: Quadrangle Books, n.d., originally published by Houghton Mifflin Company, 1924.

————. *Labor in Modern Industrial Society*. Boston: D.C. Heath and Company, 1935.

————. *The Labor Movement in the United States 1860–1895*. Gloucester, Mass.: Peter Smith, 1959; originally published by D. Appleton and Company, 1929.

Webb, Sidney, and Webb, Beatrice. *The History of Trade Unionism*, New York: Augustus M. Kelley, 1965; originally published, 1894.

————. *Industrial Democracy*. New York: Augustus M. Kelley, 1965; originally published 1897.

Westley, William A., and Westley, Margaret W. *The Emerging Worker*. Montreal: McGill-Queen's University Press, 1971.

Winpisinger, William. "Job Satisfaction—A Trade Union Point of View." Unpublished speech delivered to the University Labor Education Association, Black Lake, Mich., April 5, 1973.

Name Index